Making the most of
BEDROOMS & BATHROOMS

Making the most of

BEDROOMS & BATHROOMS

MARY GILLIATT

A creative guide to home design

St Michael

Original room designs created by Mary Gilliatt
and illustrated by Ross Wardle/Tudor Art Studios

Special photography by Jon Bouchier and Jessica Strang

This edition published exclusively for
Marks and Spencer plc in 1983 by
Orbis Publishing Limited
20–22 Bedfordbury
London WC2

Printed in Italy

CONTENTS

Bedrooms and bathrooms are the rooms in which we are supposed to relax our bodies, restore our energies, and take comfort. In short, they need not be just for sleeping, for storing clothes, dressing, bathing, washing and shaving.

So there is no reason – especially given the general shortage of space – why bedrooms should not be on 24-hour duty, used for working in as well as sleeping – and for watching television, listening to music, and even for eating; a small table for leisurely breakfasts and comfortable little suppers could be a great luxury.

Bathrooms too – given the square footage – can be multi-functional. Some people deliberately turn a large bedroom into a comfortable bathroom/study/dressing/exercise room, keeping a smaller room for actual sleeping. But even a very small room could probably be made considerably more luxurious and comforting than it is at present.

The first priority in any bedroom or bathroom, whatever its use, should be comfort. In the case of bedrooms this is not just a comfortable bed and bedclothes, although they are essential since we spend one-third of our lives in bed – but also really good lighting. And that means good to make-up by, good to read in bed and work by, good for general dressing and easy on the eye. You will want comfort underfoot too. If ever there was a place for carpet, or at least generous rugs, the bedroom is that place. Heating too, should be well regulated so that the temperature can be as good for sitting in as it is for sleeping. Quiet is an essential. If you live in a busy area or over a much-used street, you will certainly need to consider fabric-covered walls as well as carpet and multi-layered window treatments, if not double glazing, all of which will help to deaden outdoor sounds.

Bathrooms too, need good lighting and heating and warm, non-slip floors. Some kind of ventilation, e.g. an extractor fan, may be necessary to combat condensation. Handgrips on baths might seem a small detail but it is an important one if you have children, elderly people or invalids to consider.

Whether you do it all at once or aim for a series of staged improvements will depend on your budget and your circumstances.

If you are planning bedrooms and bathrooms from scratch you are lucky, because with a very limited budget you can decide your priorities and plan sensibly to achieve them as and when you have the cash. If you are hoping to improve existing rooms but cannot do it all at once you will find that even the slightest change can uplift the spirits . . . cushions on a bed, a new bedcover, tie-backs on curtains, pictures, new towels, an added plant.

The aim of this book is to define the functions of both rooms and show you how to make the best use of your available space, how to achieve an appropriate style, how to plan children's rooms so that you do not have to keep on spending as the child grows up, how to plan storage, lighting and heating, and how to choose the best furniture and equipment or improve what you've got.

Most importantly, it aims to show you how to fit your rooms to the way you live; how to make them really work for you. After all, bedrooms and bathrooms are, or should be, the foundations of your personal comfort. They deserve to be well-planned.

This splendid bathroom-cum-study, en suite to the bedroom glimpsed beyond, shows how the original function of such rooms can be extended. The mahogany colour of the desk and blind is cleverly repeated in the lining to the fabric at the four corners of the bed.

BEDROOMS

Most people would like, and indeed need, to think of their bedrooms as more than just a place for sleep, storing clothes, dressing and making up. In today's world the bedroom often has to be office, study and second living room as well. The ideal would be to have a desk as well as a bed, an armchair or two and a couch, generous bedside tables and storage, bookshelves, television, stereo, space to stash away a sewing machine and an exercise machine so that they do not spoil the elegant harmony of the whole. There should also be space for storing impedimenta like files, records, tapes and sewing stuff. Space in fact, to ensure that the bedroom really is a room for quiet and rest, a room away from the family for pursuing your own interests and work, and above all a room for comfort.

Alas, the reality is that most bedrooms are far too small for most people's ideals and need to be meticulously planned if they are to hold more than the minimum of a bed, a couple of bedside tables, clothes storage and a chair. Almost everywhere, except in roomy country or suburban houses and old-fashioned mansion flats or apartments, bedrooms are sacrificed for the greater good of the general living space. Cottage bedrooms, small flat bedrooms, new house bedrooms, conversions and bedsitting rooms all suffer from lack of the square footage that is desperately needed for real comfort. And if so-called master bedrooms are small, rooms meant for children are often no more than cells fit for a couple of bunk beds.

Luckily, a number of furniture designers are now producing modular furniture that can be shaped and re-shaped to suit awkward spaces and differing needs. If you can afford it, fine; if not, you can still do a great deal with decoration and ingenuity.

Space, one cannot stress too often, is as much a matter of *feeling* spacious as of actual room measurement. If you can foster the illusion by clever and imaginative use of mirror, lighting, pattern and multi-purpose furniture (beds that have storage underneath, chests of drawers that are also

Limited colours, the wall design repeated on bed quilting, and the bed placed cornerwise, all help the feeling of space in the bedroom on the left, while the small room on the right gets its fresh look from the blue and white scheme, deep window and plants.

Three very different small bedrooms that benefit from clever use of mirror. Light colours and a wall of mirror effectively double the size of the tailored guest room, top left. Mirror tiles set on the diagonal completely cover the end wall and cupboard doors, with their clever glass handles, on the small room above. The trellis structure makes an original bedhead and gives the illusion of an airy room divider halving a much longer space. In the tiny bedroom, left, large mirrors at right angles, framed to match the handsome chest, matching fabrics and wallpaper and pale beige carpeting all produce a tranquil effect.

work surfaces; cupboards and closets that hold files and equipment as well as clothes) you are well on the way to manipulating every inch to its best advantage – and every inch well used in a bedroom really does make an enormous difference.

Adapting to partners

Adapting bachelor accommodation – whether male or female – to take a partner can be very testing. I am not talking here about the merits or demerits of feminine or masculine decoration, but rather of making room for one more person's effects. It can come as a great shock, once the all-embracing, all-forgiving 'honeymoon' period is over, to wake up to somebody else's clothes and clutter. So every possible inch of storage has to be utilized to cope with the changed circumstances and, if possible, to disguise the overflow of possessions. And all in such a way as to give each a fair share of the space, leaving no room for complaint or irritation.

Doors, and this includes wardrobe or closet doors, are often an under-used ingredient of the room ripe for conversion. Racks, hooks, the sort of spring clips used for holding brooms and cleaning apparatus can all be used to provide extra storage. Is there room for a window seat? If there is, make it one with a lift-up lid so that belongings can be stored inside.

The old-fashioned ottoman or a similar sort of chest is another good solution. Either can be put at the foot of a bed, in a corner, or under a window to provide extra seating as well as storage. If there is a dressing table think too about a hollow upholstered stool with a lift-up lid. Make as many things as possible do two jobs rather than one.

If there isn't room to add a dressing table and/or desk, think of buying three or four whitewood chests of drawers, or chests plus a cupboard and arranging them against a wall so that there is some knee hole space. Cover the lot with a long counter top, perhaps covered in plastic laminate, paint the chests in with the room and you have a desk, dressing table, work surface and clothes storage all in one.

Right: A large drop-leafed table set behind this bed acts as bedhead as well as drawing/work surface. Floor-to-ceiling open bookshelves effectively divide off sleeping from sitting/breakfast/casual eating area. The rose and cream colour scheme freshened by touches of white in light shades and chair cushions makes this multi-functional space seem light and welcoming. Long swing-armed work lamps provide powerful light when needed but can easily be pushed up and away; so can the rise-and-fall fixture over the pedestal table in the seating area of the room.

Use the window as a bedhead

At first glance there would seem to be
no hope at all of squeezing a double
bed into a room of this size—at least
with any semblance of elegance. But
by using the window as a headboard
and by covering the bed to blend in
with the walls the room looks fresh,
pretty and comparatively spacious; an
illusion helped by mirroring the door
between the wardrobes which gives
depth and extra light to the room, and
by painting the wooden floor a glossy
white. The green and white of the
wallpaper which covers cupboard
doors as well as walls, thus
minimizing their apparent size, is not
only repeated in the matching
bedcover and bolster, but echoed in
the neat white Roman blinds edged
with green and the updated rag rug
from Portugal. A nice touch is the
white edging on the bedcover which
reverses the green edging on the
blinds. Other good details to note are
the green ribbons used to hang the
miniatures either side of the bed
which repeats the colour of the velvet
chair upholstery—a nice contrast to the
crispness of the cotton; the differing
textures on the plain green cushions;
and the way the deep window sill and
reveals are used as bedside table and as
a convenient base for mounting the
pair of adjustable brass Billy Baldwin
lights. The chest at the end of the bed
holds spare linen and blankets or
duvets as well as making a useful extra
seat/bookshelf. There is even room for
a dressing/writing table.

Above: Bookshelves tucked under a window sill and permanently drawn-back curtains make a handsome bedhead as well as solving an awkward space problem in this small room. Billy Baldwin wall lights provide the answer to where to put lamps when there is no room for bedside tables. A blind ensures privacy.

Left: Two built-in closets act as supports for bookshelves as well as providing guest bed/sofa space in this nicely book-lined work room, which also includes a desk and more shelves along the opposite wall.

Making room for guests

Today's tight spaces rarely allow for a spare room and rooms used exclusively for guests are practically non-existent in most current homes. More often than not the guest room is where the sofa bed or convertible happens to be, and it could be anywhere – in the living room, study, den, dining room or a convenient alcove in the hall. Happily, good hospitality is more a matter of *how* you accommodate your guests than *where*.

However, with a little careful planning and foresight you can make space for a guest almost anywhere in the home. If, for example, you have a sofa bed in the living room you could arrange to have a cupboard or closet in the hall which can be cleared enough to take visitor's clothes. If you can make a bed in the hall the same storage would naturally apply. If there is a sofa bed in a study, den or dining room you could try to fit a built-in closet in that room which would in any case be useful for other storage.

Most living rooms will already have a floor or table lamp and a small table which can be moved close to the sofa bed. All you need do is add books, a carafe of water or bottle of mineral water, a glass, generous towels and clean, tidy bathroom space and you are well on the way to making a guest feel just as much at home as in a self-contained bedroom.

Tricks for stretching space

When you are planning – or re-planning – a room remember the following well-tried space stretchers and see if you can apply any of them to your own particular situation and needs:

Mirror used at right angles to a window and, if possible, all along one wall, will make a room look twice as big and twice as light. A huge old mirror used as a bedhead will appear to double the space, particularly if the mirror reflects a window.

Flooring with a diagonal design will make the space seem larger, so will most geometric designs.

Using the same print on everything – walls, windows, bedspread, upholstery – will deceive the eye about the real size of the room and, by making you forget about limits, edges and boundaries of walls, seem to enlarge the space.

Disappearing wardrobes will appear to increase the wall space. Make them vanish by decorating them the same as the walls so that they don't stand out. Better still if you can merge the wardrobe frame with the walls *and* cover the front with mirror.

Screens can hide a multitude of unsightly but necessary equipment (like filing cabinets, if you use the room for working in) and at the same time give the illusion of space because of their angles.

Light colours make surfaces retreat. Use them on ceiling and floor and choose light backgrounds to fabric designs.

A platform will virtually give you two rooms for the price of one, so if you are able to plan a room from scratch and need to expand a comparatively small area, it's useful to know that you can do this.

The use of mirror always increases the feeling of space and light. It is particularly effective used at right-angles to a window to give the maximum reflection of light.

Shelving at the top and bottom of the bed can make an enormous difference. A low shelf at the foot can hold tv, stereo, books, magazines and could provide extra seating as well. High shelving at the top can act as bedhead as well as being used for books and general display purposes. If you build out such a storage and display wall a short distance from the wall proper, you could use the space behind as a study/work area.

Putting the bed in a corner or even in the middle of the room rather than against a wall, often makes the whole space more generous.

Uplights set in one or two corners of the room will make the space seem much bigger at night because it will bounce light up and soften the hard edges.

Small chests of drawers either side of the bed instead of bedside tables will make better use of the space.

A highish bed will free the space underneath for storage.

Cupboards and closets that go right to ceiling height will press into service all that otherwise wasted space, and cope with things that aren't used a lot and need to be out of sight most of the time.

The window used as sort of bedhead and curtains combined will save space in a very small room. Or if you have two windows, use the space in between for the bed.

An unused or unusable fireplace can provide extra storage: fit some shelves across the space and, if possible, a door in front.

Storage built around the bed will free the rest of the room and make it look much more open.

Use mirror panels at right-angles to a window to create an illusion of increased space and light

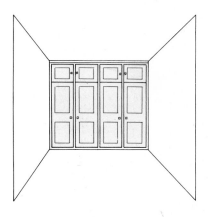

Build cupboards that go right up to the ceiling to make walls look longer and provide more storage

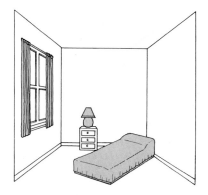

Position the bed at an angle to the corner of a room rather than flat against a wall

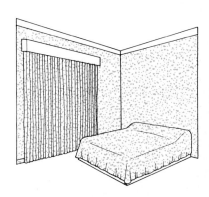

Use the same small print on a light background for walls, curtains and bedspread

dark blue velvet ribbon
gives distinction

panels and bed head
edged with blue

border gives
definition to
unruly angles

*Attention is drawn away
from the awkward angles of
the room to the left by the
pretty cornflower and white
colouring, against which the
pale furniture and matting,
soft festoon blind and skirted,
lace-covered table all take the
eye. While above, another
blue–white room is given
definition by plain blue
edging on door panels, the
cushioned bedhead slotted
onto a blue-painted pole and
the blue china jardinière.*

transparent perspex table
and glass lamp take up
no visual space

pale matting
adds textural
interest

skirted table
gives softness and
width to space

Of course, you are not limited to sofa beds. You might include a Murphy bed as part of a storage wall in the living room or study. (When shut up it is an innocent-looking cabinet – when down a bed pulls out.) Or there are deep armchairs that become single or double beds, stacking pillows or cushions or covered blocks of foam that pull together for night duty, as well as folding beds that can be hidden behind a screen or stored in a cupboard.

If you do have the luxury of a spare or guest room try to make it the sort of bedroom you yourself would enjoy staying in. Make sure it is pretty, cheerful and clean, with comfortable beds, good lighting, plenty of dressing table space, and if at all possible, a desk or writing table of some sort together with a comfortable chair. If there is a fireplace you could hardly do better than light it for guests; or have a gas flame fire.

Most important of all, try out a guest room from time to time yourself to make sure everything works and is in good order.

Right: A sleeping alcove lined and curtained with washable cheesecloth, and a matching archway, make brilliant use of space in the hallway to accommodate guests. The rather austere grey of the carpet and bed base is softened by the pastel patchwork quilt and heaped cushions.

PUTTING STYLE INTO THE BEDROOM

Bedrooms are obviously very personal. They are not on show to outsiders like the living room and can, therefore, be as idiosyncratic, or as fanciful as you like providing that they are quiet to be in and, I repeat, comfortable. If you have a good mattress, a window and some space to play with there is practically no limit to the way you can decorate a bedroom.

Most people, once grown up, have some sort of idea of how they would like their ideal bedroom. If you had a room all to yourself through childhood, or at least from adolescence on, it was the place where you spent hours reading, did your homework, thought great thoughts, made plans, practised an instrument, played music, experimented with make-up, hair and clothes styles, entertained your friends and was, in general, a real refuge. You may have been lucky enough to have had a free hand with its decoration, or you may have had to put up with the same old wallpaper and hand-me-down furnishings, but either way you would have evolved a deep gut feeling for the sort of room you would like to have, given an absolutely free rein.

When it comes to the crunch, of course, and you do have your own place, the bedroom is often the last place to be decorated, or at least decorated in the way you had imagined. But this is almost invariably from lack of funds rather than lack of ideas. People might be short on plans for living rooms but everyone can give a ready opinion on a bedroom.

What's your style?

There are clearly both very feminine and very masculine bedrooms at either end of the scale with compromises for couples made in between. But there are no rules and, interestingly, you often find in the most otherwise modern of households that the main bedroom has been decorated in a traditional way. Old brass, painted iron and pine bedsteads have made a tremendous comeback over the last decade or so. Now too, the

Red and white with strawberries on quilt and pillows, flowers on sheets and walls, add up to a clean, cheerful country bedroom, left, in contrast to the red on red print used for tented ceiling, walls and bedspread in the fantasy-style sleeping alcove of the converted barn, right, which is deliberately sophisticated.

four-poster bed has become popular again, whether it is the real thing, a modern version of the same, or an approximation devised with fabric. Half-testers – beds with a canopy which only overshadows the pillow area; filmy drapes attached to a corona; back hangings – all these are currently much in vogue.

All the same, there are certain general styles which are firm favourites and can form a framework, if you like, within which you can incorporate your own personal touches and ideas.

Cottage-in-the-country style rooms with brass or pine beds or pretty fabric bedheads, pine chests and wash-stands; lace or broderie Anglaise or both combined with fresh mini-prints, co-ordinating plains; and stripped floors either covered with rugs or stencilled.

Prosperous Victorian style bedrooms with mahogany or brass beds or fabric four-posters with either a couch or chest at their feet; ruched or Austrian blinds, pelmeted and tied-back curtains; handsome carpets and equally handsome furniture.

Edwardian style bedrooms with brass or fabric-covered beds, possibly with muslin or lace hangings or drapes, dressing tables with muslin skirts and a wealth, as they say, of silver or ivory-backed brushes, combs, mirrors and boxes; probably

prettily flower-printed walls, and again, filmy pull-up curtains or festoon or Austrian or just white holland blinds; a period fireplace and an overmantel.

Real English style would be a mixture of both the above with flowery glazed chintz, probably with leaves and roses, or leaves and birds, deep carpet, deep, maybe well-worn arm chairs, nice mahogany or painted furniture, an imposing bed, lots of cushions, books, prints, pictures and memorabilia. There would be a desk complete with writing paper at the ready and, of course, pretty little posies of sweet-smelling garden flowers everywhere.

Thirties style with perhaps a limed-oak bed or polished mahogany, or a sumptuous Hollywood-style up-holstered bedframe; perhaps Jazz Moderne rugs on a carpet, a whole bedroom suite to match the bed and all kinds of 30s details – lamps, cushions, vases, bedspreads – probably collectors items.

French country style might be small flowered patterns: flowered on walls and ceilings, matching fabric on bed, windows and chair covers. This can look splendid in a tiny room with pine, cane or painted furniture, and fruit or flower prints framed in bird's-eye walnut or fruitwood.

Fantasy style could be done entirely in fabric with a fabric tented ceiling,

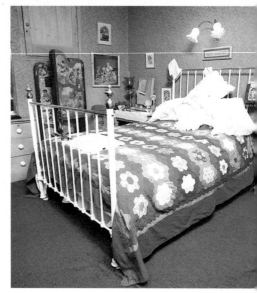

Top left: English eclectic style where practically anything goes as long as it's comfortable, pretty and well-flowered. The modern pine bedside table is quite different from the delicate 19th century bamboo and lacquer dressing chest, but the effect is still charming.

Bottom left: True Edwardiana with drooping lace, lots of wicker and elaborate silver frames.

Bottom near left: A late Victorian bedroom with William Morris-like walls, brass bed, early pine furniture, memorabilia and charming 19th century scrap screen. Only the bedspread is modern though it has the proper old-fashioned air and look to it.

Right: Difficult to define in style, this bedroom could be called prosperous but updated Victorian, or just prettified Mid-Atlantic. The half-tester with its mellow lining matching the eiderdown has two different scales of pattern in the same subtle colouring. The shawl on the upholstered stool blends gently with the cool greys of the dhurrie rug, and the frilly, lacy cushions are matched by the beautiful lace tablecloths. All nicely set off by the soft wicker chair and squashy basket.

Left: American Country, and how, with its display of rosettes strung along the mantelpiece, primitive paintings and its Colonial post bed complete with obligatory quilt. The window is always given interesting treatment, here elaborately pelmeted curtains. Upholstered chairs complete this mellow roomful of comfort.

Above: Tailored style with a hint of Japanese, visible in the screen above the bed and the collection of porcelain on the shelves. Colours are muted and disciplined. Furniture lines verge on the severe.

or a fabric four-poster with elaborately shirred top, padded fabric walls, padded bedhead, generously gathered flounce or bedskirt and masses of pretty, feminine cushions, frilled or trimmed with lace, round tables with luxurious skirts and over clothes; or all in Indian mirrored-fabric or lace, with bamboo or mirrored furniture.

American Country style could have a nice Colonial post bed with an old quilt – perhaps in one of the traditional American patchwork designs – polished floors with rag rugs, filmy lace curtains and interesting window treatments, comfortable chairs, good reading lights, naive portraits and masses of cushions. Or it might have a fabric four-poster lined with, perhaps, a check cotton with matching curtains and blinds, ribbon rugs on stripped floors.

Tailored style would be quite the antithesis of all these. Walls might be covered in suede wallcovering or felt or just dark paint or hessian, perhaps given a neat border of brass or contrast fabric of some sort. If there is wallpaper instead it might be dark and geometric. The bed would be neatly tucked with a tailored piped bolster. The window might have Roman blinds; furniture and possibly doors would be mahogany, wardrobe doors would be very well-appointed with interior lighting and mahogany linings.

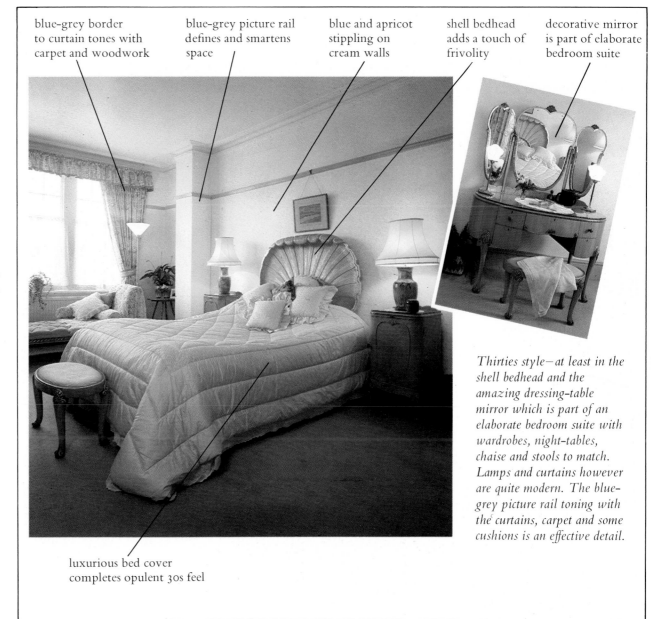

blue-grey border to curtain tones with carpet and woodwork

blue-grey picture rail defines and smartens space

blue and apricot stippling on cream walls

shell bedhead adds a touch of frivolity

decorative mirror is part of elaborate bedroom suite

luxurious bed cover completes opulent 30s feel

Thirties style—at least in the shell bedhead and the amazing dressing-table mirror which is part of an elaborate bedroom suite with wardrobes, night-tables, chaise and stools to match. Lamps and curtains however are quite modern. The blue-grey picture rail toning with the curtains, carpet and some cushions is an effective detail.

23

Adapting to partners

How to make an essentially feminine room look a little bit more masculine, or at least more asexual, without changing all the furnishings is a problem that faces a great number of couples. And of course the same problem can occur the other way round. In this particular case some clever juggling with colour plus a little sleight of hand resulted in an entirely different look. The only costs involved were for the new soft furnishings and the re-vamped junk couch at the end of the bed. To achieve this turn-around in looks, the ceiling was painted a pale, pale apple green and walls were covered in green felt superimposed with strips of red painted beading to give the illusion of panelling. The white carpet on the floor was exchanged for a green one, old quilt tablecloths were swapped for deep green velvet, and the lace-edged bedlinen was replaced by green, red and white checked sheets with a tartan throw-over and a red corduroy valance. The pink-lined white curtains were ousted by green felt Roman blinds with hardboard pelmets covered in tartan, and the same tartan was used for cushions on the white painted wicker sofa at the end of the bed. Final touches were green-painted woodwork to match blinds and walls and the white mantelpiece 'marbled' with paint to give the room a slightly more study-ish air. Most accessories, paintings and plants were left in exactly the same positions but the room is hardly recognizable.

Bed treatments

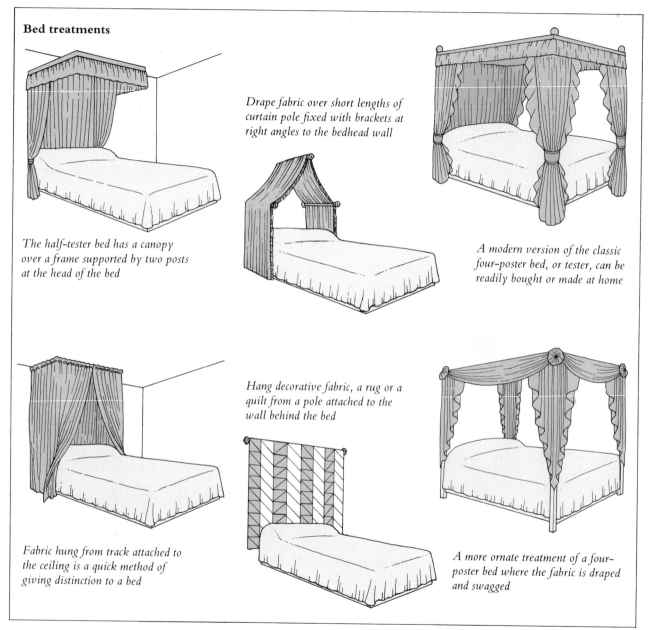

The half-tester bed has a canopy over a frame supported by two posts at the head of the bed

Drape fabric over short lengths of curtain pole fixed with brackets at right angles to the bedhead wall

A modern version of the classic four-poster bed, or tester, can be readily bought or made at home

Fabric hung from track attached to the ceiling is a quick method of giving distinction to a bed

Hang decorative fabric, a rug or a quilt from a pole attached to the wall behind the bed

A more ornate treatment of a four-poster bed where the fabric is draped and swagged

Bedroom-workrooms should manage to integrate a good working (as opposed to writing) desk and all the necessary files and clutter into a peaceful, relaxing bedroom. On the whole, the room would be rather tailored with carpeted floors, perhaps fabric walls, a neat bed which could easily look like, or even be, a sofa bed. Storage would cunningly have extra space for filing cabinets, bookshelves would be extra capacious to take reference works, there would be comfortable chairs and reading lights and perhaps a couch for restful contemplation.

Putting style into the basic bedroom

All the above vignettes are the ideals of course. Unless you are particularly fortunate, you are far more likely to have to try and inject some sort of style into an otherwise fairly basic room. Given that you have just about afforded to paint or paper the room, buy a good bed and carpet or rugs for the floor, what can you do to give it a quick shot of personality?

It is quite easy to make a significant difference with very few and often fairly inexpensive importations. You can add a heap of cushions on a bed, or cover pillows with pillow shams and leave them propped on top of a matching or coordinating bedspread. You might find a pretty chair in a junk shop which you could paint or re-cover the seat; or you could find an old shawl to drape across the foot of a bed or a chair. If there is room, you could get a round wooden table made up and cover it with a fabric skirt and an overskirt in a coordinating material. Add a lamp, some odds and ends, a framed photograph or two, a small plant perhaps, and the room will immediately look more inviting.

Then too, you could add a tall plant in a big cane basket, a whole lot of prints, a screen which you could either find and re-cover, or one that you've made yourself. Given the basic screen frame you could stain it mahogany and fill it in with voile or muslin shirred onto stretch wire like the Edwardians used to do. Or make your own version of a Victorian scrap screen either with traditional scrap pictures, which you can still buy, or with your own cut-outs.

Cane or bamboo chairs are cheap, light and attractive, and there will almost always be room, even in the smallest bedroom, for something of this sort. Add a pretty cushion and again you will make a difference. Attractive old bedside lights; a new mirror; an upholstered stool; tie-backs or a contrast border added to curtains, or a blind underneath; a paper border stuck all round the walls; such comfortable touches, and they are really no more than these, can make an amazing change to an undistinguished bedroom.

Left: The bedroom area of this Hi-Tech studio/loft has been divided, at least visually, from the living area by the blue-painted steel scaffolding-like structure slung just below the ceiling. The same sort of girders are criss-crossed across the window and covered by Venetian blinds.

Above: A vividly covered bed does not look out of place in this basically pine bed/workroom. In fact, it's just what the room needs.

PUTTING STYLE INTO THE BEDROOM

Designing from scratch

If you do have the chance to design a bedroom from scratch you are really very lucky, although couples might not think so after they have spent hours quarrelling about who should give in to whom about ideas! A sybarite might never have realized that he or she had linked up with a Spartan until the subject of decoration came up. The important thing, of course, is to learn how to compromise in a way that is comfortable and agreeable to both partners.

Discuss the subject thoroughly, pool your ideas, look around, see what you can afford and what you must discard and don't be afraid to take your time. If the bedroom is to be the restorative room it should be, then it is worth spending a long while to get it right. If you need to buy a bed, buy a good one, and a rug, and hang your clothes from hooks until you have worked out the best furnishings and methods of storage to suit you both.

If you do not have to consider a partner you are in luck again, and if you do not have to worry too much about a budget you are luckier still, although it actually helps to have the supporting framework of a limited budget. It immediately cuts down on the available choice and actually encourages you to compromise, to be ingenious, to think up new solutions which make for a much more

personal room in the end.

If you have no very set ideas on what you like, then the best thing to do, as always, is to buy what books and magazines you can, and go conscientiously through the pages marking the rooms that appeal. Or it may be that you like one idea here, another there. Note them all, see what you can afford, and go from there. There really has never been such a choice in co-ordinated wall-coverings and fabrics, bedheads, lamps, carpets, blinds, china, rugs and bedlinen. And don't forget that sheets can make splendid curtains, bedhangings and table-cloths.

Style with comfort

As I have said before, comfort should be the overriding theme of any bedroom. Of course, standards of comfort vary. What is comfortable for one, is suffocating for another. Some people are only comfortable with soft opulence; others thrive on simplicity and firm lines. The important thing to remember is that whatever style of room you choose, make sure that everything in it functions in the best possible way. Mattresses should be the best you can afford; storage should be really functional; lights should be the correct height and intensity for reading, bed linen should be comforting and beds should be easy to make.

Real comfort and style depend as much as anything else on the small

touches. The little details that count are things like inconspicuous but capacious waste paper baskets; containers of tissues and cotton wool always to hand; carafes and glasses for water, or bottles of mineral water; nicely lined drawers and cupboards complete with sweet-smelling sachets; curtains and blinds that pull easily and fit well. Some people like to wake up with a chink of light, others most decidedly do not, so try to determine this in the beginning. If you are having curtains

specially made for you, ask for them to be made light-proof, and be sure to stipulate this right at the beginning. If you possess curtains that are not sufficiently light-proof, consider putting up black-out blinds behind them, or ordinary roller blinds lined with black-out fabric. People often forget in the first rush of enthusiasm for romantic, filmy curtains, that the same fabric is not nearly so romantic during a cold night in winter, or first thing in the morning after a particularly late night.

Starting over again

If you are sick and tired of your old bedroom but cannot afford to start over again, don't despair. Go into action with one or two or more of the instant improvement suggestions mentioned earlier. A new wallpaper alone might do wonders. If that's too expensive, add one of the new borders around the room, or superimpose a fabric border, stuck with an appropriate adhesive.

A crisp, pretty new bedspread or valance wouldn't break the bank and there has never been a wider or more exciting choice around than there is now. If you hate throwing things away that still have life in them you could always cut up your old spread to make cushion covers or move it to another room.

A stunning and dramatic way to change the look of the whole room is simply to give the bed an entirely different treatment by making a fabric four-poster or half-tester or interesting back hangings.

Even changing your old bedside tables for two skirted round tables introduces a softer, more romantic look. If you have not got a tv in the room try bringing one in for your own private viewing away from the family; or add some bookshelves and more pictures, or a comfortable chair, stool or desk if you can afford it and have the space. The bedroom really is the easiest room to alter with the minimum of effort and expense.

Left: Mirrored alcoves and an all white room look luxurious, though the treatment is simple and fairly inexpensive.

Above: A skirted table to match the curtains, blue and white china and a blue painted wicker chair make this room instantly more romantic.

Right: A neutral scheme is given immediate impact by converting the standard double divan into a handsome draped four-poster.

29

GETTING THE FRAMEWORK RIGHT

Any problem is easier to solve if you can break it down into various components. It is the same with the decoration of a room. If you think – in the case of a bedroom – of walls, floor, ceiling, windows, bed, furniture, fabrics, and – last but not least – lighting, and then take each of them in turn, deciding what you can and cannot do, the whole exercise becomes very much more simple. It helps too, to commit it all to paper in the form of a check list which you can refer to and revise as you go.

Although most people would obviously think of the bed as the most important ingredient of a bedroom, it is still necessary, as in any room, to get the actual framework (walls, ceiling, floor and windows) planned out in detail even if it can't be done all at once. If you cannot afford to complete the whole room right away, at least knowing what you hope to do will help you avoid the sort of mistakes and compromises which could spoil the final look.

Walls and ceilings

Bedroom walls can either be painted, papered, or covered with fabric (or wood, or carpet, or some other covering if you are daring). Three things will guide and affect your choice: the position, condition, proportion and shape of the room, your existing furnishings and your budget. Although ceilings are very often neglected, the same applies to them, and they can make an enormous difference to the look of a room.

Paint

Paint is generally the cheapest way to cover a wall as long as the wall is in good condition to start with. If it is not, you should make it good and at the same time find out the cause of any stains on walls or ceiling and have them dealt with. If walls are merely uneven and the house is old and in the country, you might actually like to keep a slightly bumpy look. Or you might prefer to disguise the defects with an alternative wallcovering such as paper or fabric, which will cover a multitude of sins.

The fern theme gives unity to the bedroom on the left. They are printed on the creamy wallcovering, repeated in the cotton blinds, window seat and valance and woven into the lace tablecloths and bedspread. A nice bare room, right, where wood predominates and blue paint provides impact.

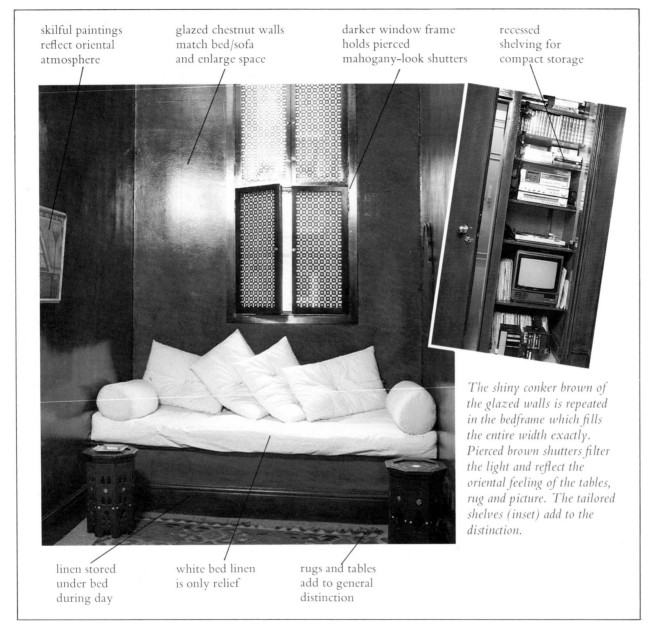

skilful paintings reflect oriental atmosphere

glazed chestnut walls match bed/sofa and enlarge space

darker window frame holds pierced mahogany-look shutters

recessed shelving for compact storage

linen stored under bed during day

white bed linen is only relief

rugs and tables add to general distinction

The shiny conker brown of the glazed walls is repeated in the bedframe which fills the entire width exactly. Pierced brown shutters filter the light and reflect the oriental feeling of the tables, rug and picture. The tailored shelves (inset) add to the distinction.

Colour counts If you do decide to paint, the next thing to consider is colour. If you want to put the focus on the furnishings and have a laid-back, relaxed scheme, choose neutral tones: soft white, soft cream; pearl grey, sand, camel or blush pink. Woodwork and ceiling could be white, or you could paint them the same shade as the walls if you want the space to seem as large as possible.

If the room receives little or no light, choose a warm colour, unless you are prepared to keep white walls very white all the time which means frequent re-painting. Make sure there is plenty of clear colour in the room as well: pinks, greens, apricots or yellows, with a lot of mirror and sparkle. One of the most spectacular bedrooms I have seen was mostly white, but the white curtains were lined with rose, there were white and rose cushions on the bed, great pots of marguerites in baskets, and above all the flicker of flames from a gas flame fire – the fireplace, of course, being a splendid extra bonus. All white-on-white rooms, pristine and beautiful as they can be, are really only good in a hot and sunny climate or in a well-staffed household. Dark walls can be restful in a bedroom. I once had a dark room with an off-white carpet, ceiling and wood-work, and the room always seemed to trap the light within itself in some mysterious way, mostly because the brown was sandwiched between very light colours. Darkish tones can also make a room seem much better funished than it is: dark green, dark rose, chestnut, dark blue, are all sophisticated and will give incidental colours used with them much more of a glow in contrast.

Finishing touches Painted walls can be pepped up in a variety of ways. You could add one of the many new paper borders just under the cornice or cove if there is one, or just under the ceiling if there is not. Or you could run a contrast fabric or webbing border (to match curtains say, or carpet) under the ceilings, around doors and windows and over the top of skirtings or base boards.

You could make your own panelled effect with lengths of beading or picture framing stuck on the walls in rectangles or squares or both. Framers will often sell it by the foot if you ask, and it comes in natural wood (paint it to suit your scheme), gilt and silver. If you can first work out the panels to scale on a plan of the room, so much the better. If not, at least draw it out on the walls carefully with a long ruler, chalk or pencil, and use a level. When this has been completed the 'panels' can be painted in a contrast of a darker or lighter tone to the main body of the wall.

Another idea is to make a dado, again with picture framing or

Top left: This heavily beamed and joisted room at the top of an old warehouse building was made light and charming with a simple coat of all-white paint.

Bottom left: An abstract pattern of yellow and blue allied to Indian cotton bedspread and cushions and an Indian carving makes the most of what could have been an unprepossessing space.

Top right: The walls were panelled out with carefully painted lines to make this room look larger and more distinguished.

moulding or even something like a double border of grosgrain ribbon. All you have to do is to run whatever frame you have chosen around the room at dado height about 90 cm (3 ft) and fill the space below with contrast paint, or paper.

Alternatively, you can try out one of the many decorative finishes like rag-rolling, stippling, dragging, colour washing, shading, glazing or lacquering which have now become fashionable again. Clear instructions for all these techniques can be found in Jocasta Innes's excellent book *Paint Magic* (Windward/Berger Paints) or my own book *Decorating on the Cheap*.

Wallpaper

Quite apart from softening the look of a room wallpaper is also an excellent disguiser of awkward angles, architectural imperfections and wardrobes or closets which might otherwise break up the harmony of a space. It is also, of course, a splendid unifier for rooms that seem all doors and windows since the paper design will link the unbroken areas together, especially if woodwork is painted in one of the colours of the paper.

There is such an enormous choice of wallpapers now in every sort of scale, colour, design and price, many of them with their own co-ordinated borders, 'partner' papers (for alcoves, behind bookcases etc.)

Painted tendrils of flowers wind their way round walls, window frame and cotton blind in an otherwise all-white room, top left. Paint is used decoratively again, top right, in this yellow-ceilinged and carpeted room where painted graphics add further interest to an already colourful scheme. Swags of painted stencilled flowers on doors, bed curtains and border, bottom left, are echoed by stencilled garlands on walls and bed linen. A painted green landscape brings an element of surprise to a formerly rather dull room, bottom right.

Left: Green and white mini-print wallpaper and a matching border make the most of a tiny space which is dominated by a decorated pine bed and knitted patch quilt. The useful storage hampers under the bed are repeated in larger scale by the wicker laundry basket. Notice the build-up of colour in rug, towels, plants and cushions.

Top right: Wallpaper and paint have been cunningly used in this bedroom. The ceiling looks twice as high and twice as interesting with its two-tone, two-scale wallpaper and paper border separated by white painted mouldings. Walls are in a paler version of the same paper with mouldings on wardrobe doors picked out in white.

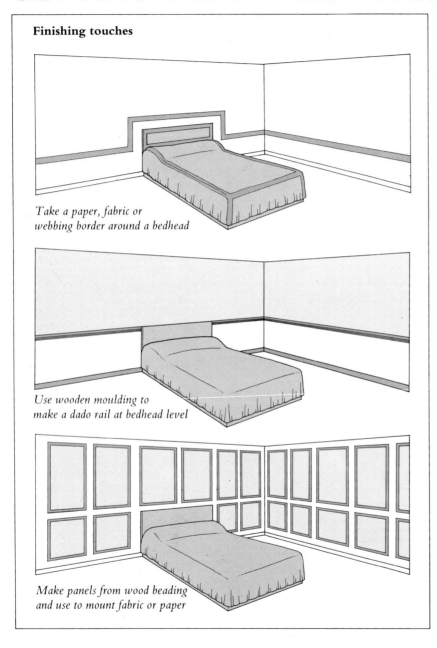

Finishing touches

Take a paper, fabric or webbing border around a bedhead

Use wooden moulding to make a dado rail at bedhead level

Make panels from wood beading and use to mount fabric or paper

and fabrics for an effortlessly unified look, that the problem is rather eliminating the unsuitables than finding the right ones.

Small rooms can be made very much more interesting by using co-ordinated or matching wallpapers and fabrics for walls, ceilings, windows, soft furnishings and the bed. The repetition of a single pattern, the use of the positive and negative of a design, or different scales of the same pattern, will add immediate distinction to a space and an all-over flower design for example, will add instant summery freshness to an otherwise dingy area.

How to cheat with wallpaper
What happens if the particular paper you've set your heart on is hopelessly expensive? Don't abandon the idea. The answer is to cheat a little. You could have it, or at least the effect of it, by painting your walls the background colour of the paper with matt paint, and then using the paper itself in panels. By doing this you can get away with the minimum number of rolls – maybe only one if your room is not very big. Or you could use a small amount of paper up to dado height in much the same way as I suggested with paint earlier on.

At the other end of the scale, cheaper wallpaper can be made to look much better and will last much longer if it is given a coat or two of matt or eggshell polyurethane –

allowing the first coat to dry thoroughly before adding a second. The polyurethane will yellow the paper a little, but this often has the happy effect of making it look more mellow, and certainly more practical since it can then be wiped clean with a sponge or damp cloth.

Preparing the walls If there was a previous wallcovering it may need to be stripped off before you start with the new. Old wallpaper can only be left if it was well put up in the first place, that is to say butt-edged with no lumps, bumps or wrinkles. If you are putting up a vinyl covering, any old paper will have to come off first. Likewise any old vinyl wallcovering must always be removed before putting up new paper. Any previously painted walls must be free from grease and dirt otherwise the adhesive will not work. So wash the walls down with water mixed with detergent or household ammonia, and for a really professional job, line walls with good quality lining paper before applying your wallpaper.

Fabric wallcoverings
Fabric walls are particularly appropriate in the bedroom for their look of softness and luxury and for their sound and heat insulating properties. There are a good many specially treated fabrics, some of them paper-backed and flame-

proofed, sold especially for the purpose, the most common being felt, hessian or burlap, suede fabric, wool, silk, moiré, grasscloth, linen, cotton and denim, all of which should be spot cleanable.

But it is quite possible to put up just about any fabric, fixing it in position by one of the following methods:

Sticking Firmly woven fabric, which will deter any adhesive from seeping through the weave, may be stuck to the wall like wallpaper. The adhesive must be applied to the wall, not the fabric.

Stapling Use a proper electric staple-gun and choose materials with the sort of design which will help to conceal seams. If you can line the walls first with Dacron padding so much the better: the effect will be very like the soft, upholstered look of battening but achieved with far less trouble. Seam the fabric first before you start applying it. Any frayed edges can be covered with a matching, contrasting or co-ordinated braid, or lengths of picture

Cool greeny-grey cotton is here gathered on rods fixed just below the cornice and just above the skirting. The top of the lace-edged Austrian blind is gathered to match, and the general softness is repeated in the generous fall of the flowered cloth.

Fabric techniques

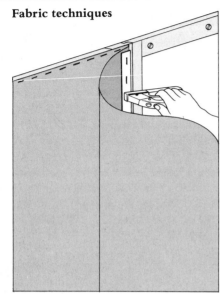

Fabric stapled over battens

Fabric may be staple-gunned either directly to the wall or stretched over wood battens which have been previously screwed into the wall

Fabritrack is an almost foolproof system patented for fixing fabric to walls which requires neither glue, nor battens nor staples

Fabric hung loosely from poles provides instant drama and is easy to put up and take down

Gathered fabric stretched between curtain tracks, fixed immediately below the ceiling and above the skirting board, looks luxurious

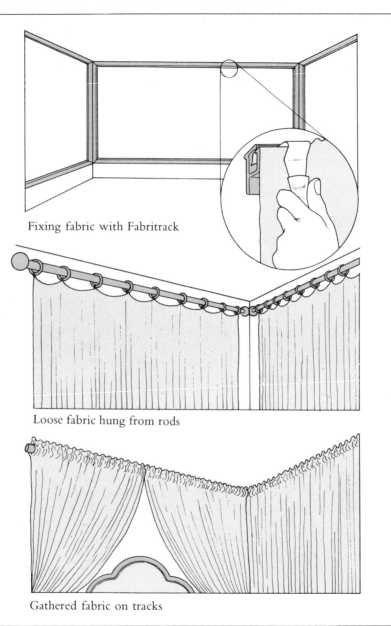

Fixing fabric with Fabritrack

Loose fabric hung from rods

Gathered fabric on tracks

framing, or strips of brass, chrome or wood beading, depending on your taste and pocket.

Clipping with Fabritrack This consists of lengths of track which you can fix all round the wall just below the ceiling and above the skirting or base boards. The seamed fabric is clipped into the track at the top and stretched down to be clipped into the bottom track. It is practical because fabric can be taken down for cleaning, moving or just changing.

Walling or battening Upholstering a wall, or 'walling' or 'battening' as it is called in the trade, means stretching pre-seamed fabric over strips of thin wood or battens which have been lined with wide strips of Dacron padding. It is somewhat complicated, but well justified by the final result. It looks professional and luxurious and, in addition, its double layer helps to muffle sound and preserve heat.

Probably the best way to do it is to staple the battens horizontally, just below the ceiling or mouldings and just above the skirting. Take vertical strips of wood cut to the size required (i.e. the height from skirting board to ceiling) and fix them at metre (three foot) intervals all round the walls. If you plan to have paintings or prints on the wall, work out where their positions are likely to be and fix your battens in these places. Remember to make provision for wall-fixed lighting, sockets, and switches at the same time. When the fabric is up the battens can easily be felt through it and hooks or nails hammered through in seconds.

Thumb tack the Dacron padding between the strips, then stretch the fabric and tack it to the battens. Cover the tack marks with lengths of braid which should also be used round the top and bottom of the fabric and around doors and windows to hide frayed edges.

Hanging Hung fabric looks especially soft and appealing when draped on the walls like curtains and is a useful method when money or time – or both – is short. It's good for temporary accommodation since the fabric can be taken down and moved. It can also be cleaned very easily since it can be removed from its fixings and put in the washing machine or sent to the cleaners.

There are several ways of hanging it. Very light (and inexpensive) fabrics like cheesecloth, muslin, or cotton can be shirred onto stretch wire or long thin poles attached just below the ceiling and just above the skirtings or baseboards in much the same way as fabric is fixed onto those nice old-fashioned fabric screens. Heavier fabrics can be suspended from more substantial poles, either shirred, or from rings, and left hanging loose and just touching the floor. Catch fabric back over windows (use blinds underneath) and doors, fireplaces and wardrobes or closets and either cover any bits of wall thus exposed with matching wallpaper if it exists, or have extra short bits of fabric in those areas.

Be different, be daring
Although paint, wallpaper and fabric are the most popular wall-coverings for bedrooms there is nothing to stop you using unusual alternatives. Quilts or bedspreads for instance, can look very exotic – Indian cotton bedspreads make marvellously inexpensive wall-coverings if you can get matching, or nearly matching ones – or what about rolls of bamboo or oriental matchstick like the kind used for blinds – or even a series of blinds themselves let loose and hung side by side if the ceiling is fairly low and the blinds are long, or if you have a picture rail.

One of the simplest ideas is to use double sheets which are in any case the cheapest way of buying a lot of seamless fabric. Or you can buy sheeting by the metre (yard) in a wide range of beautiful colours and patterns. Even carpet, or fake fur if your tastes run to it. I once saw a bedroom entirely lined with sheepskin on ceiling, floor and walls and the effect was like a woolly igloo. All these alternatives can be coverings stapled or stuck according to the weight of the material.

Plain and patterned Indian cottons have been used to line this sleeping alcove, along with bordered Indian bedspreads. Ceiling and wall fabric have been stapled onto battens and stretched. Bedspreads used as curtains are pulled across a bamboo pole for privacy at night. By day the alcove becomes transformed into a comfortable, stylish sitting area.

Floors

On the whole, I think, bedroom floors should be soft, or at least have rugs by the bed, as much for comfort and warmth underfoot as for reducing noise.

If your choice is carpet, be sure to choose the right grade, usually described as bedroom grade; it does not need to be of the same hard-wearing quality, and therefore high price, as carpet for the living room, hall and staircase. In a guest room, you can get away with an even less hard-wearing carpet unless you have a perpetual stream of guests. If you feel you cannot afford carpet for the moment you can always compromise temporarily with extra thick felt topped with rugs to distribute the wear and tear. Or it might be worth while considering carpet tiles which are comparatively inexpensive, and can be taken up if you move.

If you have a wood floor in good condition, it can be stripped, sanded and polished, or bleached to a much paler colour and then adorned with rugs. Wood in not particularly good condition could be painted or painted and stencilled and again given rugs where necessary. Pick up a colour in the curtains or walls, or paint the floor a neutral colour, like white or cream or bluey grey or – very popular in America – Indian red or terracotta.

As long as you coat the paint with a couple of coats of eggshell polyurethane (left to dry a good twelve hours in between each coat) you do not need to use expensive gloss or enamels. Give the boards a couple of layers of undercoat tinted with the final colour and you can get away with just one coat of flat or eggshell oil or alkyd (oil-based) paint. Alternatively you could use yacht or deck paint for a denser effect.

If you feel like stencilling painted floors it should be done before the final coats of polyurethane. Various shops, including the Paperchase chain, sell stencil kits complete with a charming choice of designs and detailed instructions by Lynn le Grice. You could also cover old boards with vinyl tiles or sheeting or linoleum, especially if you livened it up with inset borders or a patterned inset of your own design.

Top right: Vividly-painted floor boards, tone with equally vivid bedspreads, and rugs echo the paintings in a painter's colourful room.

Bottom right: Large striped cotton rugs tone well with the quilts on wall and bed and the decorative cushions.

Far right: White carpet and matching white wool wall covering make a luxurious background for the tailored black and white bedspread, curtains and right-angled unit furniture.

Bringing the garden in

If you find it difficult to decide on a particular colour scheme for your bedroom, or to come up with some sort of theme, see if fabric, linen or carpet designs will spark off ideas. Since there has never been such a choice of all three as there is now, inspiration and good starting points should not be hard to find. Here, for example, a delicately pretty sweet pea cotton on a trellis ground suggested that white vinyl silk walls should be covered in natural garden trellis, and the rest of the room's colours should be taken from the cotton design. Sweet pea curtains tied back with thick white cord were backed by white Holland roller blinds and given pure white gathered pelmets matched to a white valance. A sweet pea, quilted and lilac-edged bedcover was teamed with white *broderie anglaise* bedlinen trimmed with pink ribbon, and a round table given a toning pink cloth. A small bedroom chair was covered in beige cotton to match the trellis and piped in white with a white cushion. The addition of a green and cream woven carpet lent an air of freshness to the whole room. Add a bunch of sweet peas in season, a bamboo headboard and a neat white Parson's table and you can have the pleasant illusion of sleeping through perpetual summer nights – or at least of bedding down in a particularly comfortable and delightful conservatory.

Windows

Few of us have beautiful, elegant bedroom windows; sometimes they are downright ordinary but quite often they are just unusual enough to present problems when it comes to decorating. Whether you have bows, bays, casements, dormers, skylights, sloping or otherwise oddly shaped or proportioned windows, explore all the possibilities of curtains, sheers, blinds and shutters before deciding on the treatment. There are all sorts of decorative tricks you can resort to to overcome awkward or ugly windows and which will actually transform a negative feature into a very positive asset.

Windows worth looking at

Bedroom windows can be treated to look as romantic, as spare or as chaste as your taste, circumstances and the actual shape of the window – and its view – dictate. If a window is unusually beautiful or just plain unusual, it might be better to show it off rather than hide it with curtains. But you will almost certainly want some sort of covering for it in a bedroom, for even if you are not overlooked you might well want to block out the light occasionally. In this case it would be better to have a blind or café curtain which would still show off the frame and shape by day. Alternatively, translucent (but

not see-through) screening could be used if you only want occasional privacy.

Blinds and shades

Blinds might be the plain roller variety, or the more tailored Roman blinds which fold up on each other in flat horizontal pleats, or the softer festoon, or Austrian blinds or pull-up curtains or balloon blinds. All

these last five categories have vertical tapes through which pull cords are drawn to raise and lower the blind or shade. Or again, there are Venetian, bamboo, matchstick, pinoleum or vertical louvred varieties. In fact, whatever your style or require-ments, there's a blind to match them. If there is nothing particularly extra-ordinary about the window or windows, and, let's face it, there very

Top left: Elegantly ruched Austrian blinds with gathered headings soften the rather harsh modern windows in an otherwise tailored room.

Top right: Shiny olive green painted shutters add just the right subtlety of colour in this Mediterranean-style room. Note the nice change of textures introduced by the creamy crocheted cushions and plant.

often is not, but you have a radiator under the sill which you do not want to cover, or a piece of furniture there like a desk or dressing table or even the bed itself, you could still use a blind rather than short curtains. Or if you want to be really lavish and like the look of it you can use blinds with dress curtains, or curtains proper which can be elegantly arranged and tied back either side. This sort of treatment will make any window look soft and graceful and will help to cut out any unwelcome morning light which could otherwise intrude around the edges of the blind.

Incidentally, if morning light is a problem, or if you work at night and have to sleep during the day make sure that the fabric of your blinds is backed with a black-out material of some sort or Milium. And if somebody else is making the blinds for you, inform them right at the start that you want black-out backings. It is pretty well impossible to laminate black-out material onto already-made roller blinds and cumbersome to do it on all other finished varieties. In any event, festoon or Austrian or pull-up curtains only really look good in light filmy fabrics, so if you want that effect have them in conjunction with properly lined and interlined curtains that can be drawn across on top of them. Or have them with concealed black-out-backed roller blinds that can be pulled down underneath beforehand.

Blind identikit
Blinds are a useful adjunct to window decoration, whether used on their own or in conjunction with curtains. They come in all kinds of textures, sizes and prices ranging from the relatively inexpensive pinoleum or matchstick and bamboo, through Venetian and vertical louvres to the more expensive custom-made fabric varieties.

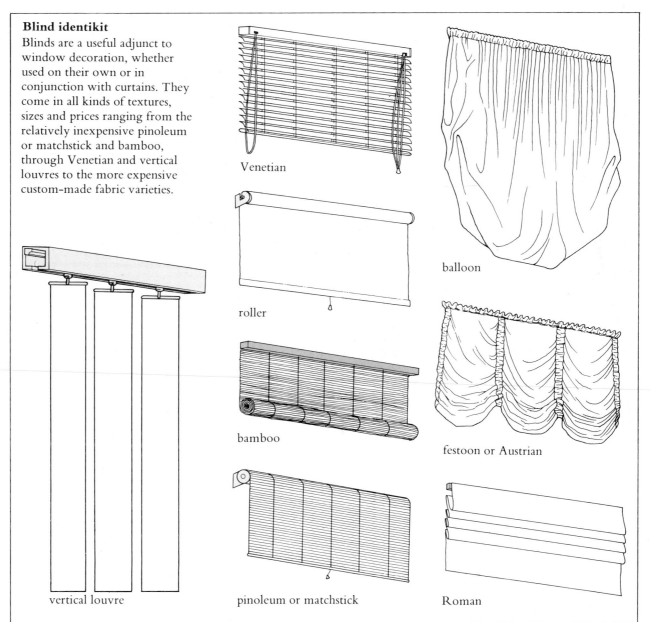

Venetian

balloon

roller

bamboo

festoon or Austrian

vertical louvre

pinoleum or matchstick

Roman

GETTING THE FRAMEWORK RIGHT

Create an illusion

It is quite easy to change the look and apparent proportion of windows by the sort of window treatment you give them. These are some of the tricks you can use to deceive – and please – the eye.

To make a window look taller Fix the curtain track or rod 15–20 cm (6–8 in) above the top of the frame. This is most effective at night when the curtains are down over the track. If you have a deep pelmet fixed about 20 cm (8 in) above the frame, the windows will always look taller during the day as well.

To make a narrow window look wider Choose a wider track or rod than the window frame so that curtains hang either side of the frame instead of overlapping any part of the window. This will also let in more light.

To make an over-tall window look shorter This is not often necessary, but if it is, put up a deep shaped pelmet or gathered valance, which will distract the eye from the expanse of glass.

To make a wide window look narrower Let curtains meet in the middle and loop them back at the sides with tie-backs or cords or deep ribbon.

To make a small high window look larger You could raise the height of the floor below by making a platform. If this is too complicated, hang café curtains on a pole which is wider than the frame.

To make the most of an arched frame Try to fix a curved track, pelmet or valance to follow the contours of the window. If this is not possible, put up a pole or track high enough and wide enough to allow curtains to clear the frame during the day.

To do without net curtains If a window faces on the street so that you need privacy but don't like the look of net curtains think of using a roller blind which pulls up from the bottom, rather than down from the top. This way you will get both light and privacy.

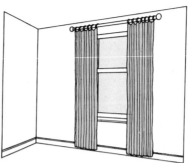

To make a narrow window wider hang curtains well to either side

To make a window look taller fix track well above the frame

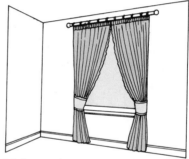

Make a wide window narrower by making curtains meet

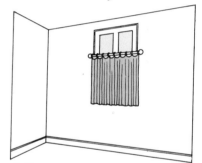

Café curtains make a small window bigger

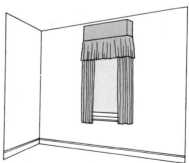

Deep pelmets shorten a too-tall window

Up-pulling roller blinds are a good alternative to net curtaining

Choosing curtains

To get the best value and effect from your curtains it's important to bear certain points in mind: be generous with the amount of material – it's fatal to skim; line them and if possible interline – they'll hang better and keep out unwanted light and draughts; get the length right – they should either reach the floor or the sill, nothing in between. (Short curtains are best kept for tiny cottage or attic windows.) Then go for the sort of curtain treatment that will be in keeping with the general style you are aiming for in the room.

The romantic, country look For this you might want rather heavy formal tied-back curtains in lace, muslin or net. Or you might decide on billowing floating lace curtains, or fresh broderie Anglaise over a more substantial holland roller blind.

Pelmets of all sorts seem to be making a come-back; deep gently-gathered fabric pelmets or valances, which might be edged or bordered, over tied-back curtains in a flowery print can look charming. A real pelmet is usually fabric-covered board or buckram, or a smooth stretch of fabric; soft, gathered tops are known as valances.

Creamy-white gathered curtains are here tied back over plain white roller blinds in a monochromatic room where the emphasis is on texture.

Top: White Austrian blinds under white curtains frame a sea view.

Above: Short chintz curtains look right in a cottage room.

Right: An attractive window seat.

The cottage look Sill-length curtains have an immediate cottage feel. They could be frilled along the leading (inner) edges and tied back with ribbons perhaps, or used in conjunction with either a gathered café curtain, or a café curtain on a pole for slightly more importance. If windows are very tiny, and the rooms rather dark, as happens frequently in old cottages, it might be better to hang a blind just above the architrave so that no light is shut out or wasted during the day. Alternatively, you could do away with any sort of curtain or blind and use the window like a picture frame to encapsulate the view. With equal simplicity you could just have a vase of flowers, a plant, a single stem in a glass, or some sort of pretty object on the sill and leave it at that.

The tailored look If you use curtains in spare, tailored, rather masculine rooms they could be in tweed or corduroy or woven wool hanging from a wooden or brass pole. But these sort of rooms might look best with roller or Roman blinds which could be edged or given a double or inset border. Crisp vertical blinds would also be in keeping, or wooden or Venetian blinds in an aluminium finish for real slickness.

Saving money – saving time
Custom-made curtains and blinds can be expensive because you are paying for labour, expertise and fabric. Ready-made on the other hand, are about half the price, come in a huge choice of colours, designs and styles, unlined, lined and sometimes thermal-lined and can be bought, taken home and hung up within a day. The only problem is that they come in standard sizes and while this is not a problem with the width it does often affect the length. This can sometimes be overcome by adding a deep border in a contrast or co-ordinating fabric and making it look intended by adding tie-backs in the same material.

Obviously, you get what you want and save money by making curtains and blinds yourself and there are now numerous books to tell you how to do it, but you can save time by improvising as well. Bedspreads, particularly Indian bedspreads and sheets can make excellent window coverings. All you have to do is turn over the tops to make a pocket for a rod or track, possibly add tie-backs – and hey-presto – you have instant curtains. Use the same material or bedspread on the bed for an instantly co-ordinated effect.

You do not even have to turn over the top come to that. Rods with clip-on café rings, like shower curtains, could do away with all sewing and give extra length – useful if the spreads are not quite long enough to reach the skirting board.

Shutters and screens

You are not, of course, limited to curtains, blinds or shades; there are other alternatives. Shutters and screens can make excellent window coverings and give an interesting architectural look to a room. Shutter panels can be bought louvred, in solid or open framework panels, and, in America, louvres, vertical and vaned shutters can be adjustable or stationary as you like. Open framework panels are also useful because you can insert shirred fabric, decorative glass or grill work of some kind into them. Solid panel shutters can be covered in fabric or wallpaper, painted or stencilled. If a room is rather small and otherwise broken up, solid shutters covered in the same finish as the walls will give much more unity to the space.

The Japanese Shoji screen with its black lacquered framework and translucent panels is another decorative way of letting in light without sacrificing your privacy. They are fairly widely available and can be made up by a good carpenter or handyman using, perhaps, cheesecloth or terylene sheets as the infill, and are especially useful for windows with a dreary outlook.

Hinged reversible screens which can be covered in different fabrics or finishes and reversed according to season or mood (try one side mirror, another side a colour to go with either soft furnishings, carpet or

walls) will make even an undistinguished short window look long, graceful and a decorative feature in its own right. Use them like shutters with a couple of panels on each side of the window which will meet in the middle when shut.

Shoji screens form a bed alcove as well as partitioning off the room in general in a Japanese designed room. An interesting contrast of textures and scale is made by the much coarser vertical lines of the bamboo window covering. The room seems calm and serene and when you look carefully at the various features in it you will notice that every surface has a different texture, and that, far from conflicting with each other, they, like the subdued colours, all blend into one mellow, harmonious whole.

The importance of lighting

As in all but the most functional rooms, bedroom lighting should be as good to look at as it is to see by. And in bedrooms it is particularly important that both general background lighting and specific lights for working or making-up are as warm and welcoming and restful as possible.

There are three main areas in which light should be concentrated: the head of the bed, the dressing area, and the dressing-table. It is also useful to have ancillary areas of light in wardrobes, on any side tables, beside any armchairs, and perhaps concealed behind plants or in corners in the form of uplights.

Plan ahead

Whether you are planning a room from scratch or just trying to improve it, try to have outlets or points positioned where the bed is to go, near the dressing-table, and the main room light in such a position that anyone dressing could have a clear undistorted vision in the looking glass. If you are planning on having wall-mounted lights over the bed, get them wired in before the walls are decorated. It is a good idea to

Left: Ceiling-mounted downlights are draped with flame-proofed lace to form decorative backings to these twin beds as well as to provide good reading light in bed.

Different shades of opinion: Period lamps like the art nouveau lamp, top left, and the converted brass oil lamp, top centre, are as important for the atmosphere they provide as they are functional. The third table lamp, top right, is modern but, like the other two, is decorative as well as useful. Each has been used as the focal point of a charming still life carefully echoing the surrounding objects as well as illuminating them. On the right, lighting is provided by the wall light as well as the more flexible swan-necked floor lamp, which provides good reading light both in bed and for working at the chest-cum-desk.

install dual operating controls at the same time; that is, one switch by the bed and a second one by door. It is always useful to get points put into corners of a room because it allows flexibility with uplights, floor lamps, and any other appliance that you might wish to use, like hair dryers, vacuum cleaners, a fan or extra heater.

Light for reading

Bedside table lamps should be high enough to shine on a book, but not so high as to disturb anyone else. Swing arm wall lamps placed just above the bedhead and slightly to the side are good, especially if they have dimmer switches to allow one partner to read without disturbing the other. Incidentally, in this respect there are now tiny extra lamps to keep on a bedside table which are adequate for reading or making notes in the middle of the night. Adjustable spots (again on a dimmer) or small angled lights are another solution. Table lamps should have the sort of shades that cast light downwards, rather than up.

If there are any armchairs or chaises in the room where you can relax and read, the best solution is to have either a table lamp on a small side table, or a floor standing lamp of some sort, like a brass pharmacy light, which you can move around to suit your particular needs and which does not look out of place.

Light for dressing

Light for dressing is usually the general or ambient light in a room. If the ceiling can take recessed down-lights so much the better. They will give better and softer overall illumination. If you cannot do this and have to use a ceiling point try using a Japanese paper shade, or a pretty pendant which will diffuse the light rather than emit an over bright glare. If there is no ceiling point, or you prefer not to have a central light you can either use table lamps switched from the door, or wall-mounted uplights which will bounce light off the ceiling and give a soft overall light – especially beautiful and flattering if the ceiling is white or a pale cream or pinkish blush.

In general, fluorescent bulbs of any sort are to be avoided in bedrooms, although they get better and better all the time; incandescent light is still better for clothes and make-up. However, if a room is very dark it does not hurt to conceal fluorescent tubes under valances or pelmets just over the window to give extra concealed light from the point where you would most expect it. You can have light thrown up to the ceiling and you can have light falling down onto curtains or blinds.

Light for make-up

If you have a dressing-table in the bedroom it is very important to have the sort of light fittings that will throw light onto your face. If you can have both top and side light so much the better. Strip lights on top of a mirror are not nearly so good as a down light fixed just above the dressing table area boosted by lights either side. The sort of strip that people have on top of a mirror is not really very effective, but of course it is perfectly possible to get a domestic version of the theatrical mirrors with lights all round that actresses have in their dressing rooms. Although not particularly beautiful, they could hardly give you a clearer picture of yourself. If you can, use them in conjunction with a dimmer switch, unless your face can stand up to the sort of brutal frankness that they provide when turned full beam.

Top left: Four draped pendant lights hung at varying heights give a pleasant, general light to this room as well as highlighting the collection of postcards and the desk.

Bottom left: Theatrical make-up bulbs are set into the sides of the mirror at this dramatic dressing table. Note how the expanse of mirror ties in beautifully with the glass knobs and the transparent perspex stool.

Right: A covered baffle hides fluorescent general light in this room; articulated reading lamps are poised at just the right height.

Since we are always being told that we spend a third of our lives asleep, or at least in bed, it is extraordinary how neglectful we are about actually choosing and buying a bed. People spend days fussing about what make of car to buy, its performance, potential and looks, whilst a bed, in which they are probably going to pass many more hours, rarely gets more than a perfunctory look and prod. Not that a bed is a life investment, for even the best mattress won't last for ever, but given a good choice, you should at least get a decade or so of comfortable use from it — and with care, several more years after that.

If you have had the same bed for years you should definitely take a good hard look at the mattress. Is the surface lumpy? Are the edges sagging? Are there any ridges and hollows? Can you feel the springs when you press it with your hands? If the answer is yes to even one of these questions, you should start looking for a new mattress forthwith.

The mattress matters

There are four different kinds of mattresses to choose from: foam, interior sprung or inner spring, water-filled and air-filled.

The foam variety is made from latex rubber or polyurethane which is manufactured in large slabs and cut to size. Latex rubber ones are the most expensive, but because of their high cost are scarce. High-resilience polyurethane mattresses, or mattresses with embedded thermoplastic beads give good support and last well and are usually dense and quite heavy. A lightweight foam mattress, therefore, is not usually of good quality and will not last long.

Interior sprung or inner spring mattresses are made of coiled springs sandwiched between insulating materials and usually come in two varieties: those with pocketed springs and those with open springs. Pocketed springs are individual units, coiled, compressed and sewn into calico pockets, unaffected by the compression of neighbouring springs and so particularly good for double beds with two partners of widely differing weights.

A nicely rustic four-poster made from branches in an equally rustic room, left, is set off by lace-trimmed linen. Equally imposing, right, triple mirrored arches edged in black make a dramatic bedhead.

Choosing a bed

The sort of bed you choose depends on several factors: whether you sleep alone or with a partner, your size – and your partner's size, the style and size of your bedroom.

Bed sizes Basically, single or twin beds are 90 cm (3 ft) wide by 195 cm (6 ft 3 in) to 230 cm (6 ft 8 in) long, although they can be bought in a narrower size for very small rooms. A small double measures 135 cm (4 ft 6 in) wide by 195 cm (6 ft 3 in) long, and a standard double 153 cm (5 ft) wide by 200 cm (6 ft 6 in) long. A lot of people like to buy bedlinen in the States so it's useful to know American sizes include Queen size which is 168 cm (5 ft 6 in) wide by 230 cm (6 ft 8 in) long; and King size which is 198 cm (6 ft 4 in) wide by 230 cm (6 ft 8 in) long. There is also in America a longer single bed measuring 230 cm (6 ft 8 in) and a Californian King size which is 183 cm (6 ft) by 213 cm (7 ft). You might see some English beds described as King or Queen size but these sizes are not standard over here. Remember that the length of a bed is just as important as the width; it should always be 15 cm (6 in) longer than the person sleeping in it.

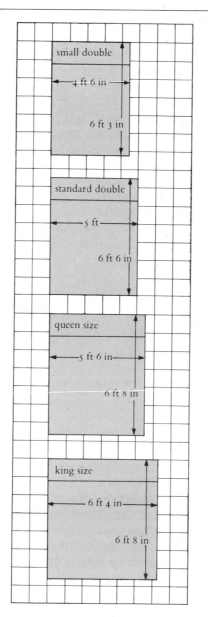

Open springs are cheaper and consist of a network of hour glass springs. The more springs there are in both types of mattress the better, and the thicker the wire the better, the number of coil convolutions the better. The best mattresses therefore, generally have coils made of low-gauge wire with six turns – lesser qualities have thinner wire and fewer turns. The springs should be covered with an insulator – to prevent the mattress cushioning from working down into the coils – and this is generally made from tough fibre padding, wire, or netting, or a combination of the three. The cushioning is usually made from polyurethane foam combined with cotton felt and other fibres, and the thicker this cushioning the higher the quality.

When you buy a mattress you should buy a partnering box spring base at the same time, it will reinforce the mattress' support and cost approximately the same amount of money. They too, have coil counts, or they may have metal grids bent in a squared zig-zag shape, or, the least expensive, be a combination of wood and foam. The foam should be at least 5 cm (2 in) thick to give any sort of adequate support.

Water-filled mattresses come in two different kinds: a sort of bladder filled with water, or a hybrid 'flotation' system which sounds, and is,

more complicated. The first type is designed to be inserted into heavy-duty framing resting on a pedestal base. The second or hybrid has a water-filled bladder which is surrounded by a foam shell, covered with conventional heavy duty ticking to look just like a normal sprung or inner spring mattress. The matching foundation is specially designed to support the water's weight. In fact, this second variety is lighter than the first because it uses less water and is shallower than the ordinary bladder type. It is also 'waveless', that is to say, special baffles reduce side to side and up and down movements of the water, and in some makes an added chemical partially solidifies the water to reduce motion.

If you are seduced into choosing a water bed, do make absolutely sure that it has a vinyl liner to contain all the water in case, dreaded thought, the mattress gets punctured. You can also get special water bed heaters which not only make the whole thing more luxurious but prevent condensation.

Air-filled mattresses are the latest thing. These are are based on the same principle as the collapsible mattresses used for swimming pools, beaches and camping. The centre of the mattress is another heavy duty vinyl sack or bladder, which is enclosed in a foam shell with a

cushioned zip-on cover like the hybrid water bed described above. Some of these air beds can be filled by means of a vacuum cleaner or even a hair dryer while others are available with a compressor unit and electric controls. Some larger mattresses have dual air chambers with dual controls to allow for differing tastes in firmness.

Does it pass the test?

The only way to tell if a mattress is right for your particular shape and weight is to try it out. Take off your shoes and lie down on it for at least ten minutes. Almost any mattress is going to feel comfortable at first but give it time and don't mind the sales people. They have got to make a sale, you have got to be satisfied. Stretch, turn over, make the sort of movements you would make in bed. A good mattress should feel firm and resilient, give support to your shoulders and hips and make your back feel thoroughly relaxed.

When you are satisfied that it feels comfortable, check the sides. They should be reinforced to prevent sagging when you sit on the edge of the bed. Sit on it and see. It should

This chrome-framed bed with its leaf design comforter/quilt and bed linen looks coolly elegant in a mirrored setting. The curved perspex table and chrome floor lamps are exactly right for this sophisticated modern room.

give a little, then spring back to shape when you get up. See if there is a cut away model on display which will show the insides. You have every right to ask to see one and the salesman should be able to explain it to you. Check the manufacturer's label which should give you complete details of construction and care. The most expensive mattresses are like the iron fist in a velvet glove, with a firm, heavy-coiled sprung core under a deeply soft top, thus providing both firm support and luxurious softness. If you and your partner prefer different degrees of firmness you can always buy different mattresses and get them linked with a zipper. Check too, about guarantees or warranties. Good quality mattresses will generally be guaranteed against defects of workmanship for some 15 years, lesser qualities for less. Good water beds, however, generally have a six to ten year limit and the heaters for three to five.

And so to the bed

Quite apart from the importance of the mattress and base there is the question of the look of the bed itself. Today you can choose from a huge range of styles from antique and reproductions of antique four-posters to specially-constructed frames with electronic controls to raise the foot and head of the bed to the occupier's fancy, or beds with

integral tv, stereo, clock, bookshelves, massage unit, lighting controls, the whole works.

If you are short of space you can get beds that fold right up into a wall of storage units (Murphy beds), or that are part of a series of slick modular units, or beds with lift-up divan bases and drawers inserted either at the side or at the end. Or there are the more straightforward sofa beds.

If you are nostalgically-minded there are shops full of originals and copies of Victorian, Edwardian and Colonial beds in mahogany, oak, brass or painted iron depending on the type you prefer. If you like a romantic look there are all sorts of elaborations that can be produced with fabric.

Bedheads

If comfort is of paramount importance to you, this will obviously affect the kind of bedhead you choose. Padded and upholstered bedheads should be attached to the bed frame and covered in some sort of easily sponged and cleaned fabric, or at least a cover that can be removed for cleaning, and it should either match or co-ordinate with the bedcovers or curtains. You could also cover a couple of squares or rectangles of foam and attach them to a wooden or brass pole behind the bed. Zip-on covers can be quickly zipped off again for ease of cleaning.

If aesthetics and looks are more important to you than comfort there is almost no limit to what you can use at the head of a bed. Bookshelves, screens, old gates, rugs, tapestries, huge posters, pin boards, windows, storage boxes, old mirrors can all be used to great effect. Use upended pillows and masses of cushions on the bed itself and you can get your comfort as well.

Dressing up the bed

There could hardly be a better choice of bed linen than there is now. Manufacturers are offering every conceivable permutation of colours,

Above: Milky-white crocheted bedspread and lacy cushions look good against the severe cane bedhead.

Top right: This brass knobbed, black painted Edwardian bed with side wings demands and gets romantic-looking lace curtains and valance.

Bottom right: Mini-flower printed duvet, pillows and curtains are teamed with co-ordinating paper and calm grey-blues and apricots in this peaceful little room.

Far right: Broderie Anglaise on a charming late Victorian bedstead.

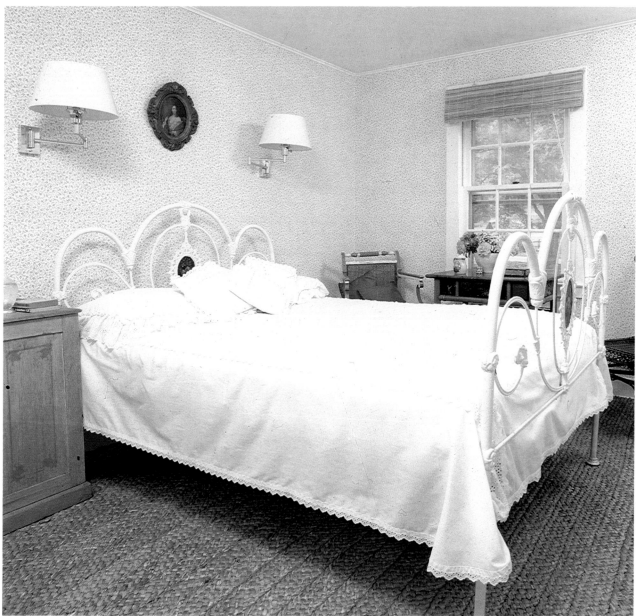

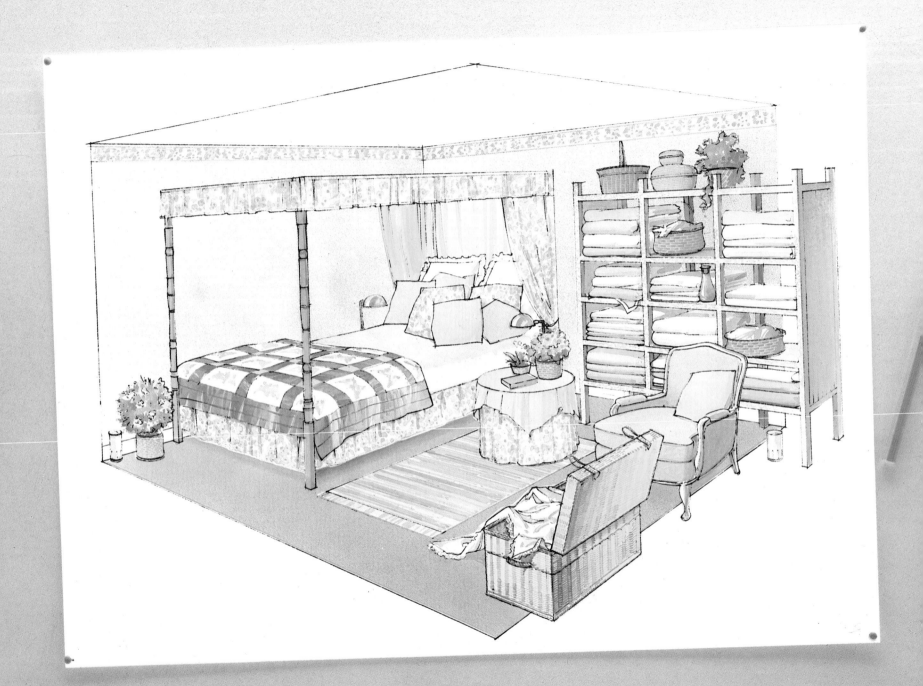

Making a choice

The superabundance of beautiful new bedlinen and the current delight in decoration for its own sake make it all very easy to achieve romantic looking bedrooms. And the choice of co-ordinating fabrics and wall-coverings now available is so wide and so good that it is quite difficult to put a foot wrong. Bedlinen itself is so pretty these days it's a shame not to display it and let it become part of the general scheme. In this room a soft blue-grey carpet and a love-in-the-mist wallpaper with its own gentle border provide the framework for a splendid wood four-poster, so well dressed it practically becomes a room within a room. Bed curtains and valance are made in a flowered cotton to match the border and are lined with swirled pink cotton. This same pink is used as a top cloth over the flowered undercloth on the table and, together with a similar blue fabric, for cushions. Sheets are pale blue with white *broderie Anglaise* pillow slips, and the whole bed is covered by a blue and white quilt. The stripy rag rug on the floor picks up the various colours and the blue chair by the wicker laundry basket repeats the blue and white of the stored linen on the shelves. Finishing touches are supplied by a pair of brass floor lamps, judiciously placed uplights, and a collection of baskets as well as plants.

Sheets as show-offs

Since sheets are both highly decorative and the cheapest way to get a large amount of fabric together for comparatively little, it stands to reason that they can come into their own in more ways than one in a bedroom. Sheeting is also more convenient to use than unfinished furnishing fabric – ideal for the non-sewer.

Use sheets –

Instead of conventional material for a four-poster or half-tester.

To make festoon blinds or balloon shades or pull-up curtains and match them up with the bed treatment (on the bed itself, swagged across the top of a four-poster . . .)

For graceful tablecloths on round tables beside the bed, topping them with a contrast sheet or lace or broderie Anglaise.

To cover armchairs and/or a sofa or chaise longue in the bedroom.

To cover a dressing table.

To make pillow or cushion covers.

As wallcoverings, hanging them direct from a rod running all around the room.

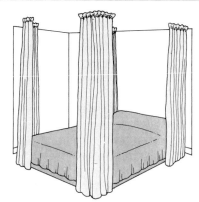
Hang sheets at the bed's corner from curtain track on the ceiling

Use contrasting sheeting to cover bedside tables

Tie a sheet around an armchair for instant re-upholstery

designs, co-ordinating sets of sheets, valances, bed skirts or ruffles, pillow cases, bedspreads, duvet covers, comforter and blanket covers and pillow shams. These last three are innovations from America which has long been the instigator of every sort of bed fashion and comfort. Pillow shams go on top of pillow cases so that the pillows can be propped on top of the matching comforter (an elegant slimmed-down eiderdown-like version of the duvet) or blanket cover (like a thin sheet-weight bedspread). And pillows come in every shape and size to be piled in luxurious confusion or profusion at the head of the bed.

Duvets, comforters or blankets?

The look of your bed will depend a lot on whether you have a duvet, comforter or blankets and bedspread. Points in favour of duvets – they're warm, light, about a quarter the weight of blankets, and they do away with bedmaking. Duvet covers are changeable, washable, highly decorative and can be matched with pillows, valances and curtains. Comforters are thinner and neater than duvets, often come with their own matching valances and pillow cases and are coming, deservedly, more and more into favour. On the other hand, many people like to feel the weight of blankets and to be warmly tucked in. It's also easier to throw an extra blanket on or off,

whereas you're stuck with a duvet, which can be too hot in summer. Comforters are more useful for year round use although duvets are now available for summer use, designed on the same principle but lighter. Duvet and comforter fillings can either be natural or man-made. Down gives warmth with minimum weight and in order of quality and cost you can choose from eiderdown (very expensive), goosedown and duck down, down and feather (51 per cent down) and feather and down. The more feathers the heavier and cheaper the quilt. These natural fillings are comfortable and settle warmly around the sleeper. They should be sent to a specialist cleaner. Man-made synthetic fillings – like Courtelle, Terylene, Dacron, Trevira or polyester with feathers and down are more moderately priced and usually machine washable – so good for children – though not as warm as a natural quilt. The categories of warmth of duvets are known as tog ratings (tog is a measurement of heat insulation). Low is 7.5 tog, high is 10.5. The one you choose will depend on how warm your bedroom is and how much you feel the cold.

Marvellous uses for fabric

Since there's no ignoring the bed, go to the other extreme and make it the most spectacular object in the room. And you can do this with fabric, achieving the most extravagant, elaborate and beautiful effects with hangings, drapes, bed curtains and canopies. If it's illusions of grandeur you're after, fabric, imaginatively used, will get you there.

● A modern four-poster in wood, brass or steel can have billowing side curtains in a light flimsy fabric like cheesecloth, voile, batiste or gingham, or be neat and tailored with straight folds of heavier fabric – tweed, corduroy or flannel.

● Attach a ply canopy or tester to the ceiling over the bed or have it cantilevered from the wall behind and cover it with fabric. Use it as a support for four sets of tied-back curtains. Alternatively, fix ceiling-mounted track around the top of the bed and hang with curtains and a valance. Curtains can be hung from small pieces of track mounted on the ceiling above all four bed corners.

● A half-tester or canopy can be attached to the ceiling just above the pillow area or cantilevered from the back wall about 1.80 m (6 ft) or so up, covered with fabric and hung with back and side curtains.

● A straight panel of fabric can be hung behind the bed, or a length of fabric can be looped over a central dowel or bracket fixed, say, 150-cm (5 ft) above the bed and then over a pair of brackets.

Using fabric to effect. In the room top left, wooden curtain rods are attached to the ceiling and hung with a valance and curtains of ribbon-edged voile to form a full tester. A very original treatment, top centre; multi-coloured ribbons are suspended in front of a panel of striped cotton hung from a brass pole. Thin blue, red and yellow lines on the bedspread repeat the ribbon colours. Crisp pink cotton is used to edge, line, and cover this white and brass four-poster, top right. The ends of the bed in the blue room, bottom left, have been upholstered in the curtain and quilt fabric, while left, voile curtains billow round bed and window.

Bedroom storage has to take care of most if not all of our personal possessions so it must be an essential and well planned part of its design. Somehow there has to be found space for all or some of the following: clothes, shoes, underclothes, hats, make-up, jewellery, personal papers, books, files, shoe-cleaning equipment, sporting equipment, bags, briefcases, luggage, accessories of every description, hobbies and the extraordinary amount of other impedimenta that inevitably ends up in the bedroom.

In an ideal world there would be a whole wall of storage behind not too conspicuous cupboard or closet doors where there would be slots for most of these things. They would all have their allotted place, would all remain tidy, and there would be space in the room for a large but elegant pedestal or bureau desk to take all papers, and shelves to take all books and other paraphernalia.

Alas, it is not an ideal world and there is seldom ideal space in a room to plan out the kind and amount of storage you would like. All the same, if you really set your mind to it and consider all the possibilities you can usually work small miracles. And

even if it is impossible to give any sort of blueprint on storage that will suit everyone, there are certain common sense methods for organizing whatever space you do have at your disposal.

How to fit it in
First and foremost, whether storage is to be custom-built, bought ready-made or somehow improvised, it must be fitted into the room as neatly as possible. Otherwise the most elegant of furnishings can be spoilt by the undisciplined welter of belongings. If you are planning a room from scratch you should take a long, detached view of storage possibilities right from the start. Take particular note of your room's proportions and architectural details. In an old building, bedrooms with high ceilings and nice mouldings might be best served with a free-standing cupboard or wardrobe. Large old pieces can often

Exposed red and white storage units at one end of this bedroom-study, left, hold stereo equipment and tv, while space-enhancing mirrored doors are used to conceal a wall of wardrobe, right, in a well-planned bedroom. Note useful two-tiered rods.

Hiding it all away

This bedroom is as much sitting room as sleeping space and so well planned is the storage that by day there is hardly a trace of the bedroom's necessities. Pine louvered cupboards built all round the room contain drawers, shelves and a dressing table area as well as hanging space, and tie in neatly with the natural louvered shutters on the window. Drawers under the sofa beds keep bedlinen and duvets hidden away out of sight and the two upholstered stools with their lift-up lids cope with anything else that has to be concealed when the sitting room is in use. For the rest, the walls are done in an interestingly textured creamy basketweave covering, the cotton of the sofa beds is a slightly mottled apricot and both colours blend happily with the soft terracotta wool of the carpet. Plain blue and white striped cushions look good against the apricot covers and so does the patchwork quilt; the blue is picked up again in odd accessories. Tall green plants either side of the window add balance and freshness to the whole.

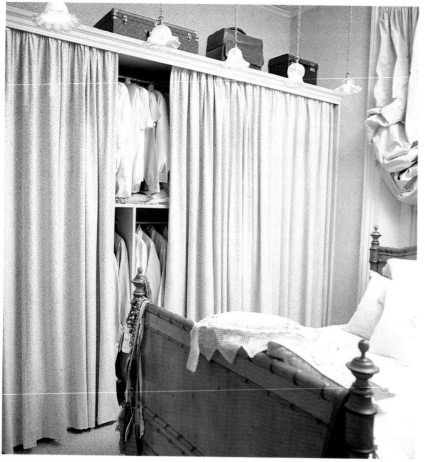

In a small room where any sort of conventional wardrobe space could look obtrusive, soft storage might well be the answer—that is to say, clothes covered or concealed by curtains rather than more rigid doors. In the room above, well-planned storage is arranged behind curtains which match the wallpaper. They are suspended

behind a piece of moulding which repeats the cornice above. The top gap—which could have been unsightly—is filled with handsome old luggage while a series of old milky glass light shades suspended from brass chains hanging in front form a kind of unusual and decorative visual screen, an imaginative solution.

be bought gratifyingly cheaply, and can often be re-organized inside to take an extraordinary number of possessions.

If you definitely decide on built-in storage (or built-in *looking* storage because most storage units are modular and can be made to look custom fitted) and you have convenient recesses or a spare wall or corner, try to ensure that the cupboards reach ceiling height and that any mouldings or base boards or skirtings that are covered are re-introduced and matched along the fronts. Few things spoil the proportion of a room so much as an unsightly gap between the top of a wardrobe and the ceiling quite apart from the fact that it is an unnecessary waste of space and a dust trap. If the cupboard is then very high you can put away your least used objects up there and reach them when necessary with a small pair of steps.

To be really unobtrusive any sort of cupboard fronts should be made to seem part of the walls and brought in with the same decorative treatment whether painted, wallpapered or covered. Wallpaper or covering should either be wrapped around the doors or brought to the edge and covered with thin beading to prevent frayed or torn or worn edging. If you give the wallpaper a coat or two of matt or eggshell polyurethane this will make it much tougher. Alternatively, wardrobe

doors can be mirrored. This can be an excellent solution especially in a small or darkish room where it will serve to expand both space and light.

If you want cupboards to look like objects in their own right they should still, if possible, incorporate some detail or feeling from the rest of the room whether it is in colour or trim or general proportion. If you decide on louvred doors, try to buy half rather than full louvres to prevent too much dust entering the slits. Panelled doors can be painted to match the room door or doors, or inset with a colour or paper or fabric that matches the walls.

How to conjure up space
Sometimes you can look at a room and feel that there is simply no place at all to put a cupboard. But look again. A wall that has one or two doors in it, for example, could have cupboards built *around* the door or doors so that you seem to walk through deep closets to the room, landing or corridor beyond. This is often a very effective way of getting good storage space without seeming to encroach on valuable room space. The same thing could be done around a window or windows, especially if you can incorporate a dressing-table and drawers as well.

Occasionally in a smallish room you can build cupboards around the bedspace with the top cupboards continuing over the bed to form a

All about storage

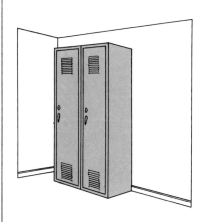

Skinny painted gym lockers make good cheap storage.

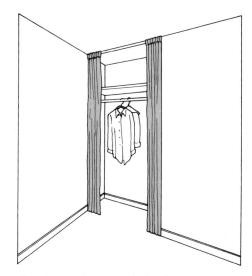

Curtains can disguise rods fixed into recesses.

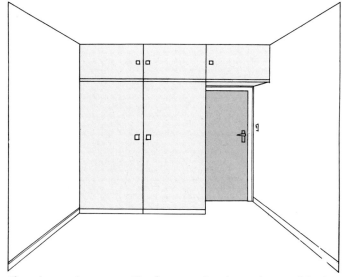

If you have a door to one side of a run of wardrobes build in another cupboard over the top of the door frame to form a neat lobby.

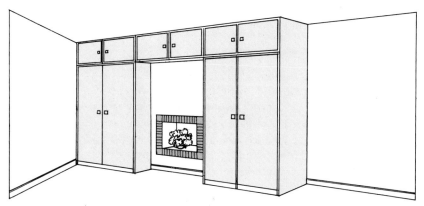

Fit wardrobes and cupboards either side of a chimney breast and run a bridge of cupboards over the top to neaten the look of the two units.

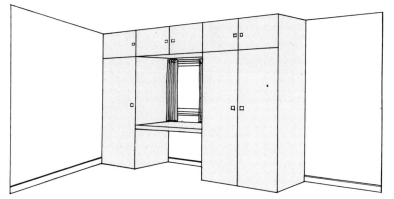

Build wardrobes and a run of high cupboards all around a window and fit a shelf across at sill level to make a useful desk-dressing table.

sort of recess. Sometimes it is even possible to fit small shelves into the sides of the cupboards to hold books, and other bedside clutter. Lights can be fitted across the underside of the top cupboards or on the side walls so that everything looks and is beautifully and neatly integrated.

If there are two windows, the space between the windows might be used either for a cupboard or shelves, or the space might just be big enough to take the bed, leaving the rest of the wall space clear for storage.

Again, you might put a bed up against the window (as long as it is well draught-proofed) which will put more room space at your disposal for storage purposes.

In a very small room, it might be best to put up cupboards in the corridor outside rather than curtail sleeping and dressing space still further.

Or a bed can be set up on a neat platform of carpeted drawers, or right up on top of low cupboards. In any event, if there is space under a bed for extra storage drawers so much the better.

Other space-saving tricks are folding doors on top and bottom sliding tracks which will take up the minimum of space when they are opened; cupboards with curtained fronts rather than doors; cloakroom racks concealed by curtains or screens as a temporary measure.

Organization and method

Whether you are building new storage or trying to re-organize the storage you have or that already exists in a new room there are certain helpful pointers to using the space to its – and your – best advantage.

For example, clothes racks are often fitted unnecessarily high so that the space below is not properly utilised. A reasonable height is 1.5 m (5 ft) from the bottom of the cupboard leaving the top part free for generous shelving space. Alternatively, you can have two banks of rods for short clothes like shirts, jackets and skirts in one wardrobe, or part of a wardrobe, and longer hanging space in another. If there are few drawers in a room but many shelves, wire or cane baskets are a good idea for keeping underclothes, shirts, sweaters, tights, socks and similar items tidy. Tie racks can be fixed to the insides of doors, so can racks or hooks for belts. Stacking plastic drawers can be inserted into any suitable space for shirts and sweaters and are especially good in clear plastic so that you can see contents at a glance. It's a good idea to store shoes on shelves one above the other rather than in a heap at the bottom of a wardrobe. Or shoes can be stashed away in one of those hanging wardrobe bags or shoe tidies for extra efficiency.

If you're lucky enough to have a whole wall of storage or a walk-in

Top far left: Industrial shelving and wire baskets hold an amazing amount of clobber from luggage to linen, clothes and general paraphernalia. A desk top has been fitted in too.

Bottom far left: A useful storage wall has been built around a door for maximum use of space. Roller blind fronts repeat bedspread colours.

Left: Brilliantly coloured and devised Hi-Tech system lets it all hang out in a decorative way.

Above: Decorative storage can be made from almost anything if you care to put your mind to it.

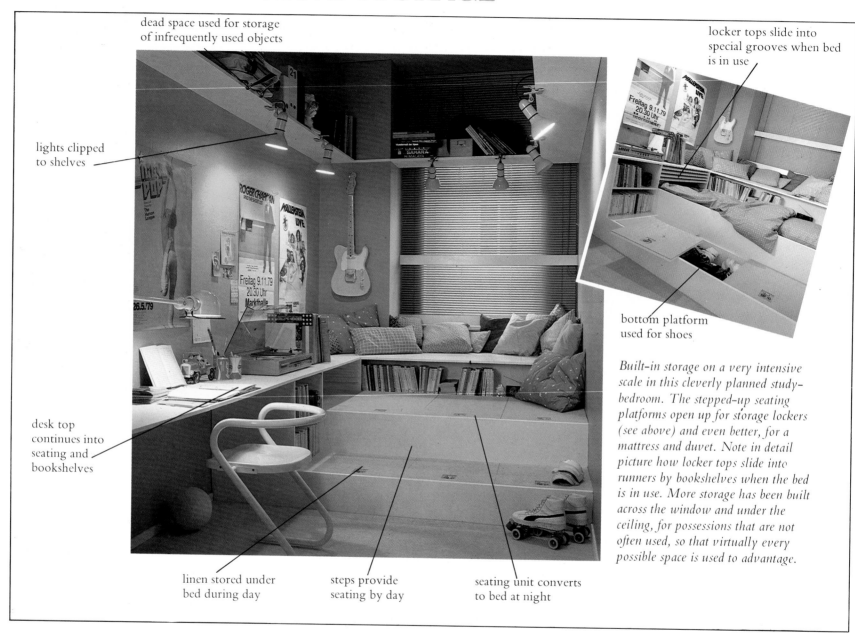

dead space used for storage
of infrequently used objects

locker tops slide into
special grooves when bed
is in use

lights clipped
to shelves

desk top
continues into
seating and
bookshelves

bottom platform
used for shoes

linen stored under
bed during day

steps provide
seating by day

seating unit converts
to bed at night

*Built-in storage on a very intensive
scale in this cleverly planned study-
bedroom. The stepped-up seating
platforms open up for storage lockers
(see above) and even better, for a
mattress and duvet. Note in detail
picture how locker tops slide into
runners by bookshelves when the bed
is in use. More storage has been built
across the window and under the
ceiling, for possessions that are not
often used, so that virtually every
possible space is used to advantage.*

cupboard, drawer or shelf space will be part of this. Otherwise you might have room for a chest or chests of drawers or a dresser. If a dressing-table is not included in a storage wall (or in the bathroom) a separate one could be used as a desk/dressing-table with drawers for papers as well as cosmetics. Another space-saving idea is to leave sufficient knee-hole space between two or three chests of drawers or 70 cm (28 in) high filing cabinets, and run a separate top over them; this gives you a writing and dressing-table surface as well.

And don't forget that most valuable area of storage space – under the bed. Drawers here can take lots of spare bedding or clothes.

Building-in the basin

If you have room for a wash basin in the bedroom, this will certainly relieve pressure on a family bath-room, and if you can incorporate it into a cupboard which can then act as a dressing-table area as well, you will have solved several problems very neatly indeed. Build the basin into a small vanity unit with a vinyl or tiled top and try to include a drawer unit, a towel rail, some hooks, electric points for razor, toothbrush and hair dryer, and, of course, a well lit mirror (one with lights all round, like a theatrical mirror would be ideal). If there isn't room for such a cupboard, a screen would make an admirable substitute.

How to improvise

If you're short of space or money or both, there are various ways to improvise quite adequate storage. A piece of wood with hooks to take hangers will serve very well as a temporary measure. Always add hooks to the backs of doors too, to take coats, dressing gowns and the odd overflow of clothes.

Cloakroom racks can be bought comparatively cheaply and can look quite decorative if they're tidily hung with clothes and left like that, or concealed by a screen or curtains. Old gym lockers can be painted and used for shirts and underclothes. Recesses either side of a chimney can be used very effectively for temporary storage by mounting dowelling or broom handles across them from which to hang clothes.

Old lace curtains hung from a brass rod repeat the feeling of the bedspread as well as concealing rather more utilitarian storage. Wood shelves can be varied to hold everything from luggage to linen. Wire filing baskets are slotted in for smaller items and the same system is stretched to form full length hanging space as well. The whole concept is as effective as it is simple.

Children's rooms – whether they are combined sleeping-cum-playrooms (which are the norm), or just bedrooms (which are a luxury), have to be capable of growing up with the child. When you are first planning the room try to keep in mind the subtle modifications you can make over the years so that with the minimum of background change – and thus expense – cribs can give way to cots, cots to beds, and toy cupboards to wardrobes and storage for adolescent paraphernalia.

This does not mean that you cannot go to town on the decoration; on the contrary, you can have great fun with this room and be as bold, as fantastic, as indulgent as you like with accessories, fabrics, storage boxes and so on. But rather that the background or framework of the room should be as simple, sturdy and classic as possible. In this way you can afford to change certain parts of it, like window treatments, bed sizes and storage without structural or expensive alterations to walls, floors and other basics.

From nursery to bed-sit
With thought and ingenuity it's possible to make the same space

work for years. Recently, for instance, I evolved a child's room which was designed to last in just such a way from infancy to late teenage. This is how I did it:

Stage 1 – Infancy The walls were painted white, and vinyl-coated cork tiles laid down on the floor for quietness and practicality. A large washable rug went on top. Machine-washable broderie Anglaise was used to pretty up the cradle and Venetian blinds were put up at the window. A white melamine trolley held the plastic bath, nappies, soft towels, aprons talcum powder, gripe water, pins tissues, cotton wool and a plastic bucket. A pair of white-painted chests of drawers with a kneehole space between and a white Formica top over the two provided a useful surface for changing the baby. A full-size wardrobe or closet with a stack of shelves on one side and a double row of

Platform-based beds, left, set at right angles and massed with cushions make maximum use of space. This cot, top right, will easily give way to a bed with no change of scheme. The deep border, cut-out figures and painted piano, right, all look fun.

75

hanging rods on the other was built in and completed the storage. At this stage the shelves were for holding soft toys and so on and the lowest rod could go on being used for clothes that needed to be hung up and continue to do this for quite some time. Final touches were a rocking chair, a few pictures and wall lights on a dimmer switch so that there would be no safety hazards once the child started to crawl and also so that the lights could be dimmed right down for minimum disturbance and maximum reassurance at night. These lights were placed near the changing area and near the cradle. A cork pin-board was added behind the Formica-topped chests of drawers for pinning up weight charts, diet sheets and so on.

Stage 2 – Toddlers and pre-school At this point the cradle was put aside and a cot introduced. This had to be both safe and sturdy which meant making sure that the slats were not more than 6 mm ($2\frac{3}{8}$ in) apart, that the rails were an adequate height for protection even when the drop side was lowered, that the drop sides themselves were the sort that could not be released by a child and that the mattress was a perfect fit with no dangerous gaps left.

The blind was left where it was as it helped to delay the start of the day, made day-time resting easier and meant that daylight could

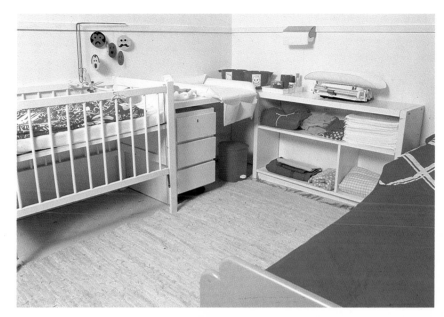

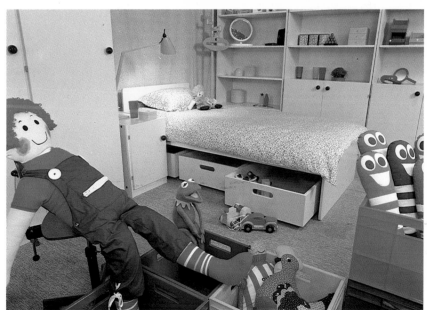

Opposite: Maximum use is made of a barn-like ceiling with contrast colour, stencilled border and Christmas lights strung along the beams.

Top left: The tops of these white units make excellent changing/weighing space that will convert later.

Top right: Diagonally-laid vinyl stripes repeat colours in Austrian blinds in this sleeping/play space.

Bottom far left: Modular units match bed with its capacious drawers and give excellent variable storage.

Left: Fun tower gives work/play/bed space.

Left: White-painted scaffolding makes an attractive bed-cum-climbing tower in a tongue-and-groove, pine-lined attic space. Candy coloured stripes and spots add to the cheerfulness.

Above: Red and white checked paper, yellow painted floor and furniture, grid shelving and red Venetian blinds are used together to make an arresting study/bedroom for a teenager.

be adjusted when necessary. An old wooden chest catered for the overflow of toys. All of the baby's accessories, like nappies etc, which were no longer needed were taken away but the trolley was left as a useful place for storing games. Some reasonably close-together vertical wooden bars, clamped into a frame were screwed into the sides of the window so that there would be no possibility of adventurous explorations onto the outside sill when the window was opened. Nor could the bars be used for climbing since they were vertical and too close together to provide any sort of head trap.

The cork pin-board was now used for pinning-up first drawings and paintings, and the walls were still able to be kept fairly pristine in spite of the ravages of dirty little hands and scribbles because white was so easy to touch up. Still, just to encourage drawings in the right place, I added a large blackboard and secured it against the wall from the floor for easy access. Bookshelves were put in.

Stage 3 – Early school days The cot went out and was replaced by a couple of modular bunk beds. These were useful in a variety of ways since they were the kind that could be dismantled and turned into two ordinary beds and also had an extra large drawer underneath for even more toy and games storage. Even

though this room was for one child, bunk beds were a good investment as they meant that there was always room for a friend to stay overnight and they provided a play area at different levels. It was safe to take down the window bars. A couple of chairs and an angled desk light were added so that the Formica top over the chests of drawers could now be used as a desk for homework as well as for painting, model-making and so on. The pin-board went on being practical and the shelves in the wardrobe were now used for sweaters and shirts instead of toys, while the top rod in the wardrobe was beginning to come into its own. The trolley became useful for jigsaw puzzles and other games and the walls were adorned with more and more posters, drawings and other memorabilia with just enough space left for a mirror.

Stage 4 – Secondary school The bunk beds came down and turned into two couch-like beds placed at right angles, with tailored covers, cushions and an extra drawer under what was the top bunk. The major purchases at this stage were a new rug and blinds to go with new bedcovers (these could be home-made), and a low plastic table to go between the beds with a bedside lamp. The trolley became an excellent base for the tv whenever it was brought in but there was no longer any need at

79

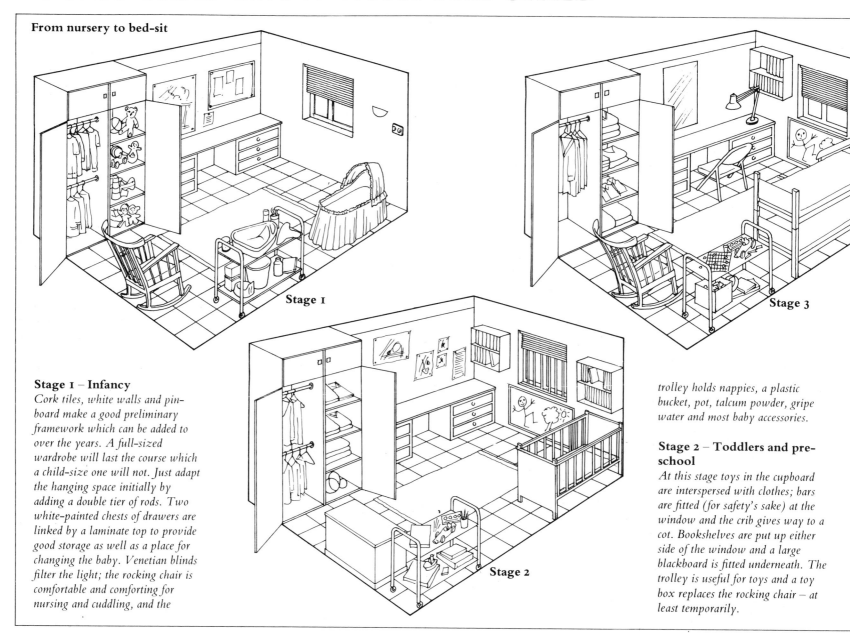

From nursery to bed-sit

Stage 1

Stage 2

Stage 3

Stage 1 – Infancy

Cork tiles, white walls and pin-board make a good preliminary framework which can be added to over the years. A full-sized wardrobe will last the course which a child-size one will not. Just adapt the hanging space initially by adding a double tier of rods. Two white-painted chests of drawers are linked by a laminate top to provide good storage as well as a place for changing the baby. Venetian blinds filter the light; the rocking chair is comfortable and comforting for nursing and cuddling, and the

trolley holds nappies, a plastic bucket, pot, talcum powder, gripe water and most baby accessories.

Stage 2 – Toddlers and pre-school

At this stage toys in the cupboard are interspersed with clothes; bars are fitted (for safety's sake) at the window and the crib gives way to a cot. Bookshelves are put up either side of the window and a large blackboard is fitted underneath. The trolley is useful for toys and a toy box replaces the rocking chair — at least temporarily.

Stage 3 – Early school days

The child is now old enough to need a single wardrobe rod and the rocking chair comes back. The trolley is still used for toys and games but the cot is replaced by bunk beds. The chest fitment now becomes a desk/dressing table with the addition of a mirror, desk lamp, and folding chair.

Stage 4 – Secondary school

Now the old Venetian blind has been changed for a smarter fabric roller blind and the bunk beds have been dismantled to form two sofa beds at right angles to each other to

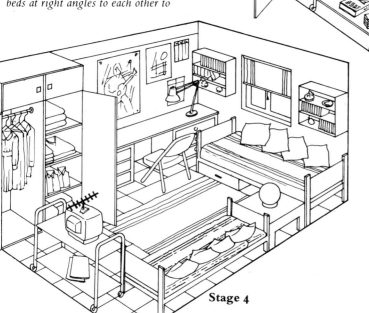

Stage 5

Stage 4

allow greater floor space. New additions are a small side table and lamp between the beds, posters, ornaments, a mass of different coloured cushions, a smart new rug – and that faithful trolley becomes a TV stand.

Stage 5 – Late teenage

At this stage the cork tiles give way to a wall to wall carpet. The pin-board is replaced by a panel of mirror and the roller blind, dirtied very quickly by early teen extravagances, is replaced by a pretty more feminine affair.

this stage for the blackboard.

The rather sculptural ladder for the bunk beds could be painted yellow and hung on the wall like a piece of sculpture along with the pop star posters and so forth, and the pin-board began to be used for school timetables, reminders and other more useful notices.

Stage 5 – Late teenage Since this particular bedroom was a girl's, I now wall-papered the walls and put carpet to the floor for a softer, more feminine look. The pin-board was taken down and replaced with more pictures and prints. Bookshelves, wardrobe, chests of drawers all stayed the same except for a coat of paint and I changed the bedcovers and cushions. By adding a table mirror the Formica shelf unit became a dressing-table as well as desk. The trolley was repainted and remained a tv stand. (If there had been room it would have been a good idea to add a small armchair at this stage. Similarly the toy chest could be stencilled and used for storage.) The room by now had assumed a totally different and pretty bedroom-like character but it had by no means been a costly metamorphosis, just a very gradual one and affordable at every stage.

Bed and playspace combined

If the room is to be used as much for playing as for sleeping – and most are

– it is obvious that every inch counts. Let's start with the bed. Once a child is past the toddling stage there are all sorts of space-saving beds which can either be used for playing and climbing over (bunks) as well as providing extra storage underneath, or can be folded up into the wall to take up the minimum of floor. Other ideas are modular beds with backs which can be used as sleeping-seating areas as well as to define space; sleep/play 'tower' structures which can also encompass storage and seating and, of course, truckle beds where one bed slides under another.

When there is more than one child it is essential to try and make some sort of private territory for each one, even if it is only visual. You can divide the room with screens or a two-sided storage unit or a low wall or even a ceiling-hung Venetian or louvred blind. If the space is fairly small, keep background colours neutral and identify each child's equipment (toy boxes, stools, chests of drawers) with a different primary colour to provide vivacity and accent and immediate recognition.

Far left: Red painted tubular steel bunk beds can be curtained off by a large blind.

Top and bottom left: More tubular steel used for beds and shelves gives work exercise and sleeping space as well as bright and useful storage.

Making it safe
Vertical bars at the window, cots that conform to proper standards, out-of-reach wall lights to prevent accidents with trailing wires and free-standing lamps – these are some of the most important safety factors to be considered during the very early stages. From here on children are more active, mobile and curious and the hazards increase. Sensible parents can reduce the possibilities of accidents by dealing with the following danger points:

See that electrical points or outlets are flush with the wall and not placed down near skirting or baseboards or within crawling reach. Keep any electric appliances well out of reach and see that cords or wires are as short as possible.

Have non-slip floors, carpet if possible – or as non-slip as possible. If they also deaden sound, especially if the room is on an upper floor, so much the better.

Make sure that fireplaces, stoves and fires of any kind – open, gas, electric – are well guarded with a childproof fireguard all the time.

Put a safety gate on the stairs and see that it is kept shut at all times as a matter of course.

See that lights are on a dimmer switch and can be dimmed right down to act as night-lights. They are also useful if you have a second baby which needs to be attended to in the night without disturbing the older child. If a dimmer switch is impractical for some reason install a low-powered night-light, and if a child remains afraid of the dark buy small illuminated plugs that fit into wall outlets and give a comforting glow for little cost.

Make or buy vertical kiddi-bars – no more than 12.5 cm (5 in) apart

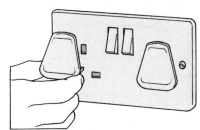

Fit covers over electrical sockets or outlets as a precaution

Use a BSI-approved safety gate to fit at the top or bottom of stairs when you are busy elsewhere in the house. They are equally effective fitted in doorways

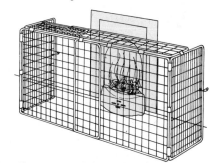

Buy a strong BSI-approved fireguard which you can attach to the wall around any fire you use

Put it away

Keeping things tidy in children's rooms unless the occupants are naturally tidy is like trying to dig a hole in wet sand. However, there are enough good storage units around at the moment to encourage a modicum of neatness. They don't have to be worthy or expensive; in fact, the more exciting, inventive and unusual they are, the more likely they are to be used. And brightly-coloured containers can add just the right touches of cheerfulness and fun to a sturdy basic room.

How to cope with the clutter

Use old school or gym lockers and paint them in different shades of bright gloss paint, one for each child if you have several. They'll take clothes or, fitted out with shelves, can be used for books and papers as well. They can be bought fairly reasonably from institutional suppliers and you can often find them in junk yards and shops.

String canvas bags and pouches on rope frames for the kind of 'soft storage' that is popular in America. Or copy this good home-made idea of a 3 m (10 ft) ladder raised on wood strips with the struts used to support home-made canvas bags in bright colours like red and blue.

Nail strips of wood 25 mm by 75 mm (1 in by 3 in) to the wall to form 60 mm (2 ft squares). Fill the insides with cork tiles, pegboard, blackboard and shelves and you have both practical off-the-floor storage and a wall that's full of interest.

Use a window wall to make an entire run of shelf and cupboard storage. Use 50 mm by 100 mm (2 in by 4 in) uprights, build them around the window, fill with shelves at different heights and support them on a row of edge-to-edge lockers or chests. The top of the lockers will provide a good play surface, the narrower shelves will hold books and toys and the lockers will house a multitude of possessions.

Fill in an unoccupied top bunk to make a marvellous out-of-sight dumping ground. Frame the sides and top by putting up painted strips of wood measuring 25 mm by 100 mm (1 in by 4 in) and fill in the gap above the bottom bunk with vividly coloured roller blinds or bamboo blinds to match whatever you have at the window.

Run a series of boxes with lift-up lids all down one wall and cover the top with long slabs of cotton – or vinyl-covered foam to make seating as well as storage units. Add bright and patterned cushions for extra comfort and accent colours.

Let them choose

Adolescents should be able to decide their own room schemes as far as it is practical – and affordable. At the very least they could be offered a number of choices so that they feel the final say-so has been theirs. Obviously they will need a bed and, if possible, a spare bed for a friend; a work-table-cum-dressing-table; at least one chair; storage space; a long mirror and good lighting for working, dressing and atmosphere. Up-lights and/or spotlights with coloured filters will add the sort of disco glamour that's often required at that age, but for the rest they can hang up fabrics on walls, paint murals, make dados, and generally inject their own character into the space without doing too much harm. In fact, fabric on walls and carpet covered by rugs are to be encouraged as good sound-deadening devices for the stereo.

Top left: Large-scale green and yellow filing trays cope neatly with a multitude of toys and clutter in a bright parrot-coloured room and encourage children to tidy up.

Right: A simple green unit with a small-scale side piece and toning diagonally striped blind makes an excellent and eye-catching work/play space in this well-equipped room.

Far right: A tiny space tucked under the eaves in a top floor flat has been cleverly turned into a two-bedded room/play area. A series of green and white cubes provide seating and storage. The diagonally striped carpet makes the space seem twice as big as it really is. Clever painting completes the grand illusion.

86

Rented bedrooms and bedsitters can be very dreary. The problem is how to cheer them up without investing too much that you'd only have to leave behind. Many landlords will not allow their tenants to repaint, knock nails into walls or change curtain fittings. Don't worry – there are ways around such difficulties.

● Cover dirty or worn patches on carpet with a large rug or rugs. You can choose from a great variety in every colour and at every price level and you simply take them with you when you move on elsewhere.

● Brighten up windows either by looping the old curtains back with cord tiebacks and adding rattan or matchsticks blinds which you attach to two hooks screwed into the window frames (fill in the holes afterwards and paint over them). Or take the curtains down altogether and just have blinds – it's neater. Put the curtains back before you leave. A third idea is to take the curtains down and put up ready-made curtains of your own, using the same fixings. Or tie the old curtains back and hang some plant baskets in front of the window to introduce some living colour and freshness to the room. Windows can get very cold so select plants like ivies, that can withstand sudden changes of temperature.

Stand big plants in generous cane baskets wherever there is a space or corner. Stick an uplight behind them for instant night-time glamour. You can take both plants and lights away with you. Add a large basket full of plants to a space beside a chair; mass plants on the window sill, and droop ivy and similar trailing plants with tendrils from bookshelves or the top of ugly wardrobes.

Hide a really ugly piece of furniture with a screen. Either buy one or just buy a frame and fill it with shirred fabric of your choice.

● Dress up the bed with pretty or stunning bedlinen – it's so well designed these days that it deserves to be shown off and can provide a real bright spot in an otherwise dull room. Pile a mass of cushions in colourful heaps on bed or chairs.

Paper butterflies, a toning rug and bedspread, and healthy plants make a charming room, left, for little cost; while, right, a cheerful miscellany of fabrics and rugs has instant impact.

When less is more

To live successfully in a one-roomed
flat or bed-sitting room you have to
be disciplined. It stands to reason then,
that if the room itself looks disciplined
and is well-planned from the start you
are more than half-way to making a
success of what, for many people, is
an unnaturally restricted environment.
In a small space less is definitely more.
Once you have decided on your
furnishing necessities (supposing you
have the choice) and come to terms
with the space you have to play with,
you should think up a limited colour
scheme – confining yourself to only
one or two colours will greatly help
to both smarten and expand the space
available. In this case I chose grey and
white cheered with touches of red. To
give as much living space as possible I
decided to invest in a wallful of units
to include wardrobe, bar, cupboards,
drawers and a Murphy bed (which
folds away behind wardrobe-type
doors during the day). I fitted white
shutters to the window, added a
chrome-and-glass desk which can also
double as a dining table and fixed an
outsize hook on the side of the
wardrobe to take more see-through
plia folding chairs. Two armchairs
covered in grey flannel completed the
furniture together with a wicker
storage basket with separate lid to turn
it into a side table. Grey flannel walls,
grey and white sheets, grey quilt
bedcover, and the red in the carpet,
cushions and rug, and obligatory plant
and floor lamp finish it off.

BRIGHT IDEAS FOR RENTED BED-SITS

● Disguise walls that cannot be re-painted or papered. Fix stretch wire all around the perimeter of the room just below the ceiling or better still, if you are frightened of leaving any marks from fixings, buy those extendable rods which will just click into place. Hem some wall length fabric at top and bottom – use inexpensive cotton, or butter muslin – thread it on to the pole or wire and either let it hang to the floor or catch it again on to similar rods or wires just above the skirting boards.

● Make your own colourful backdrops by hanging those long rolls of coloured paper that photographers use. You can get them from photographic supply stores. All you have to do is run them through the extendable rods mentioned above and let them drop to the floor. Result: instant wall colour change at the flick of a wrist.

● If disguise is out of the question, try distraction instead; some inventive colourful feature that costs little but will immediately attract notice, divert attention from other-unsightly bits of the room and also be a delight in itself. Kites, for example, like the paper dragonflies in the picture in the top left hand corner of the opposite page, will instantly provide a centre of focus. Their bright colours can be picked up in piles of cushions.

What's on screen
Screens disguise eyesores, increase the feeling of space by adding perspective, are marvellous for dumping things behind or for concealing a rack of clothes, and are generally decorative in their own right. Either make one yourself, if you are handy, and paint it, lacquer it, decorate it, stencil it, cover it with fabric or simply fill in a hinged screen with shirred fabric. An alternative is to stretch transluscent textured paper or net onto a hinged frame for an oriental look. If you can't make one, find a second-hand one and re-paint or re-cover it.

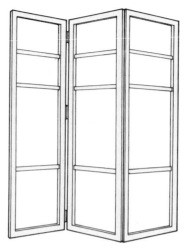

Translucent paper looks oriental

Attach gathered fabric to a hinged frame

Hinged louvered doors make a screen

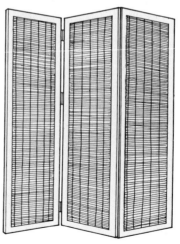

Glue split bamboo to a second-hand screen

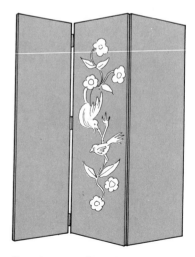

Repaint, stencil or decorate an old one

Top left: Stunning printed cushions and paper butterflies allied to pink and lavender blue immediately add character to a simple room.

Top right: Green and white checks and a mini-print make a pretty fresh little room enhanced by green paint and plants.

Right: Colourful ceramic birds and flowers surround a small Victorian fireplace and grate to give it a good deal of extra charm.

Far right: Colourful inexpensive curtains, bedspread and rug give personality and warmth to a spartan white-washed room.

I was going to say the bathroom has come a long way from the uncomfortable cold space it often was. But in fact Egyptian bathrooms, Roman bathrooms, ancient Greek bathrooms were immensely sumptuous affairs with good plumbing and a great deal of luxury. That there was a gap of so many centuries before we really began again to treat the bathroom as the healing, cleansing, refreshing place it should be is almost incomprehensible, but there it is. Once again we are taking enormous interest in the room as a room to enjoy and not just a place to house those indispensable items, the bath, washbasin, shower and WC.

Bathrooms need some deep thought of course, especially if you have the opportunity of planning one from scratch. Young childless couples, elderly couples, families with babies or teenage children, those with spare, Spartan inclinations and those who love comfort and glamour all have their differing needs. But basically the problem can always be defined and isolated by your answers to the following three questions: How much money have you to spend? How much space have you got to play with? Do you want a luxurious

bathroom or a practical, hygienic splashing place?

Practical bathrooms that come in from the cold

If you live in a modern house or block you will generally have efficient new plumbing even if the actual bathroom or rooms are given very little space, and nondescript space at that. If your bathroom is one of these and has a shower over the bath you might think of tiling it all over. Although it will be more expensive initially than painting or wallpapering you won't need any more maintenance for years to come.

Forget about tiles being cold and clinical; these days the repertoire of beautiful colours and patterns is enormous and you can always soften any hard lines with large fluffy towels in luxurious shades, with interesting window treatment and a stunning carpet. If you do want to save money

Boldly striped cotton is used to form a decorative canopy over the bath area in an interesting bath-exercise room, left. The same fabric is neatly pinned back by the shower. Stripes again, right, are used to good effect to give character to a wood-lined room.

by using mostly white or cream tiles you can insert a border of patterned tiles to run underneath the ceiling, down corners and around the bath. This will inject colour, relieve the monotony and take away any arctic feeling.

If you live in an older house or block you might trade elderly fittings and antiquated plumbing for more space. Although changing the plumbing around is a major expense – if indeed it is possible at all, you can at least change the fixtures for contemporary versions which will work a whole lot better.

For example, you might think of looking for water-saving WCs or showers which will conserve your hot water supply. If changing the fixtures seems impossibly expensive (and don't forget – you can often find second-hand baths, basins and WCs in good condition for half the price because they have been thrown out in favour of later models or different colours) think of changing the taps and shower fittings: this comparatively minor change will instantly give a more stylish look.

New baths for old

If the plumbing works well but the fixtures are jaded, chipped and stained do not automatically think of throwing them out. Baths, basins and even WCs can be renovated and resurfaced by professional firms (consult your Yellow Pages). Or

Far left: Border tiles are used to create a panelled effect in this elegant, restrained bathroom. The polished wood bath panel looks good against the mole grey carpet.

Above: A tiled partition wall divides lavatory and shower stalls in a neat blue and white room. Floor tiles have been used to form a defining border below the ceiling.

Left: A bath has been cleverly inserted here into what might have seemed an impossible space. Mirrored walls and cleverly designed storage make the most of the remaining area.

Styles for tiles

Plain white tiles are usually the least expensive type to buy. Make them look more distinguished by laying them on the diagonal, colouring the grouting with added pigment, adding border tiles to the leading edges or just below the top run, or making a checker board effect.

Use border tiles, or ordinary decorative tiles, for a decorative edge

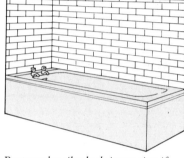

Rectangular tiles look interesting if you lay them like stepped bricks

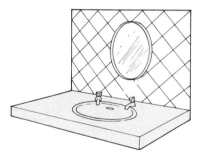

Lay square tiles diagonally and they will make the area seem much bigger

Cheer up an expanse of plain tiles by dropping in the odd decorative block

Far left: A completely mirrored wall gives a light and airy feeling to the bathroom of this tree-surrounded country house. The polished wood cabinet for the basin and the arched mirror superimposed on the larger slab of mirror look especially effective with the stripped and polished floors, the beamed ceiling and the abundance of plants which serve to link inside with outdoors.

Top: Tawny faux marble cornices, skirting boards and splashback blend well with the fabric used for the elaborate festoon blinds. They also provide an effective counterpoint to the art- and photograph-covered walls.

Bottom centre: The border on the graceful long white curtains is carefully matched to the tiled bath surround in another elegant and personal room. An old painted chair, wood framed prints and nice old hanging shelves are handsome additions.

Bottom left: Modern lozenge-shaped floor tiles look good with the classic twin basins on their sturdy porcelain pedestals, the long curtains, the fireplace with its flowers and mirrored overmantel and the painted, towel rail and chair. Although mostly white the room looks very far from clinical.

you can resurface them yourself with epoxy paint if you are handy and, above all, patient. You must first take the time to prime the original surface to ensure a really smooth slick finish when you spray or roll on the epoxy, and you must wait the requisite time (usually a day or two) before you can safely use the fixtures again.

Outsides of old baths can also be painted with a design, or stencilled to look especially interesting. It's often a good idea to have the sides built-out a little and panelled with wood so that they look both generous and contained, especially if the sides are deep enough to sit on or to put things on. Old basins too, with their sad underpinnings of twisted pipes, can also be enclosed with wood to gain respectability and provide storage space at the same time.

Plants in the bathroom

An instant facelift for an existing bathroom can be achieved by the addition of plants. Their vivid colours, plant pots and often sculptural leaf shapes can all be used to great effect for little outlay in either time or money. Moreover, the warm humid conditions are often particularly suited to certain varieties of houseplant. But remember that they need good light as well as bright direct, though not necessarily hot, sunshine. Few plants thrive in deep shade or gloomy places. Air con-

ditioning will de-hydrate them and if your bathroom has fan ventilation this will cause draughts which plants dislike. Some require constant humidity and should be stood in plastic trays on a layer of constantly moist gravel or pebbles. If your bathroom is kept at a low temperature – around 5°C (40°F) – your choice of plants will be more limited, but *aspidistra*, *hedera canariensis*, *rhoicissus rhomboidea*, *sansevieria* and *ficus pumila* are sturdy enough and should be satisfactory. Bowls of mixed plants are a good choice for a small bathroom; they take up little room but give a variety of colours and textures. Don't overwater these and remember that containers without drainage holes should have a thin layer of gravel in the bottom. Some plants, like ferns, hate drying out and some, like aspidistras, dislike dust and need to be sponged occasionally. All plants should be turned to let the light get at all sides. To avoid disappointment, only buy plants that come with good instruction labels telling you how to care for them and what sort of temperatures and conditions they prefer.

Not only but also

If it's big enough there's no reason why it shouldn't serve not one but two useful purposes. You could consider making a bathroom-dressing room, a bathroom-exercise room, a bathroom-study, or you

might add a bathroom end to a bedroom, simply screening it off. If there is room for clothes storage, either in the room, or in a lobby just outside, you can add a hanging cupboard or closet, bring in a chest of drawers, install a long mirror or a mirrored wall, insert a comfortable chair, maybe a rocking chair or an old wicker chair, put down a carpet and you will have an interesting dressing-room – especially if there is space to add a dressing-table and chair or stool as well.

Keep-fit enthusiasts might find the bathroom a good place for an exercise bicycle, a rowing or jogging machine or whatever. If all this gym equipment doesn't look particularly beautiful it could be screened off with a screen, a hardboard partition or tall plants.

One of the most interesting bathrooms I have seen was a bathroom-study with the desk and chair partitioned off from the bath area by a towel rail acting as a low divider. Shower, WC and bidet each had their separate alcoves on another wall, and the far wall was covered in floor to ceiling bookshelves with a comfortable leather chair, reading light and small side table in front of them. Even if there is no space, or more to the point, no funds to provide all this, you might still be able to provide a work table, chair, telephone and wall-fixed work light in an odd corner, or alcove.

THE BATHROOM IS A ROOM TOO

A rose-tinted bathroom
The bathroom is, or should be, a warm, cheering place, so a nice rosy glow, as in this scheme, could be very suitable. Walls are covered in a highly practical old rose vinyl which looks like corduroy, all the wood is mahogany stained, and the rose is picked up again in the carpet, which is rather darker than the walls. The bath is placed along one side wall, slightly raised on a platform and enclosed by two sets of shelves, one of which forms a separate recess for the WC. The wall behind the bath and shower is covered in rosy brown and pinky beige checked tiles which amalgamate the other colours in the room, and towels are shades of light and dark rose. More towelling is used for the cushions on the cane chair and as a shower curtain lined with plastic and hung on a polyurethane-coated mahogany pole. Other details: brass Billy Baldwin lamps either side of the mahogany mirror, the mahogany clock on the end wall, the collection of healthy plant life, and, on the bath step, the generous basket full of sponges and soaps.

porthole-like
wall lamp

red/white/blue
umbrella (for showers?)

all trims
painted blue

*Everything has a highly nautical
air in this blue, white and red
bathroom. Well, perhaps not
everything. There are two
amusing exceptions: the
Shakespearean bust to the side of
the basin, and the baskets more
pretty than shipshape. For the rest,
the room is very spruce with its
blue outlined trim, red door, pipes,
lavatory cistern and radiator,
nautical towels and its porthole-like
wall lamps. The bath is set
interestingly at an angle and
divided from the red-edged
deckchair end of the room by the
radiator. Note the life-belt.*

no window
treatment but
life belt as
decoration

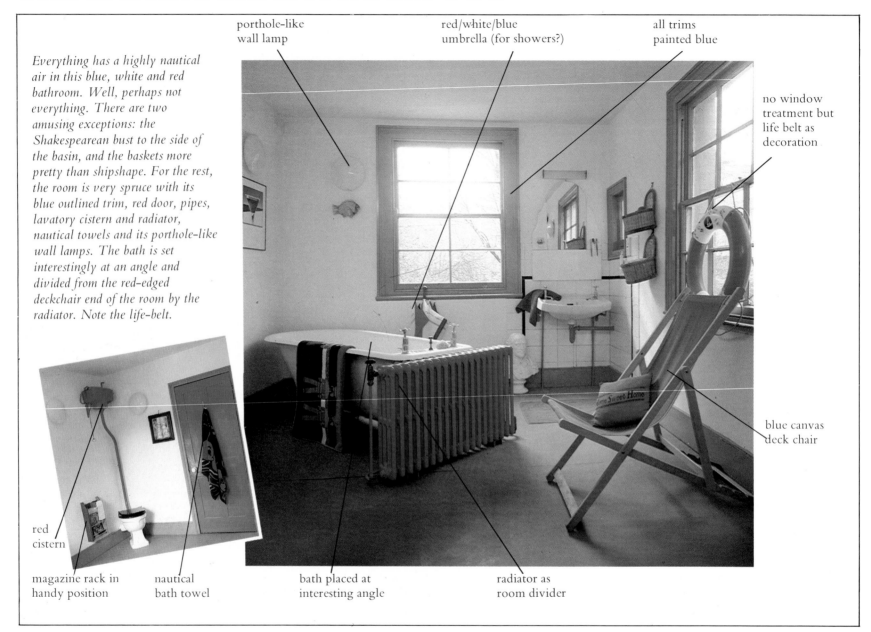

blue canvas
deck chair

red
cistern

magazine rack in
handy position

nautical
bath towel

bath placed at
interesting angle

radiator as
room divider

Incidentally, the new cordless telephones are perfect for calls in the bath and if this is where you have your inspirations, a battery operated recorder could be at hand.

Comfort on a shoe-string

My own feeling is that bathrooms should be comfortable, civilized, rather decorative, and certainly personal rooms – an ambition one can achieve more cheaply in this area than in any other part of the house bar the cloakroom or powder room. For with care, one can usually manage to achieve an air of luxury for a comparatively small sum, using expensive fabrics, tiles, and wall coverings that can be afforded here because they are only needed in small quantities. Conversely, you can of course spend a fortune, and still end up with an unsatisfactory and uninteresting space, since bathroom personality depends much more on colour, mood and accessories than on actual equipment.

Problem areas

If you inherit an existing, boring little space with fixtures that cannot be moved or changed it isn't the end of the world but it does call for positive action. There are literally dozens of cosmetic changes you can put into effect without spending a fortune. Here are some instant face-lifts that will give any jaded bathroom a new lease of life.

● *Large expanse of tiles in a colour you hate* Paint over them with eggshell yacht paint followed by a coat of gloss paint for a lustre finish, or with epoxy paint. Give the walls a good clean first to get rid of all lingering traces of dirt and grease and then apply a coat of primer. Alternatively you can tile over the top, either with new tiles or with sheets of ceramic tiles or mosaic with flexible grouting already in place.

● *Shabby walls* Put up plastic-laminated surfaces which can go over almost anything. Or panel the walls with wood, or cover them with tongue-and-groove wood coated with polyurethane.

● *Unexciting walls* Cover them with a wallpaper which might be far too expensive to use in a larger space; or with fabric or felt above a run of tiles, or at least a run of transparent perspex or plexiglass or glass around bath or basin.

● *Uninteresting room* Paint the walls a dark rich colour and use them as a background for prints, drawings,

Right: Black-painted tiles, black carpet, smart black and white border, and black and white towels make a very dramatic space out of this small room. Gilt-edged prints and the red brass-trimmed blind add elegance; the plaster cast feet and the plaster bust of Nefertiti provide the right extra balance of white as well as humour.

Left This small bathroom was made to look extremely pretty at very low cost by painting every surface white, curtaining off the bath with white lace-curtains and adding plenty of plants.

Above: Fabric curtains are used to conceal the storage area below the set-in basin in this graceful bathroom.

Right: Mirrored ceiling, side walls and bath panel give interesting illusions of grandeur to this actually very small room with its burnt-poker-wood finish.

photographs, collections of this and that, memorabilia, whatever you fancy, in order to add lots of interest and impact.

● *Dull dark room* Paint everything white from top to bottom, white tile or sheet vinyl the floor (white carpet would get dirty too quickly but you could put down easily washable cotton rug) and mass every available space, including the window embrasure with plants. This will make even the dreariest little room look fresh and airy.

● *Cramped space* Don't forget the power of mirror. Panels will open the most confined space even if you only mirror the back of a door.

● *Ugly windows* Pretty them up by covering horrible obscured glass with a permanent blind in flimsy fabric or put up café curtains – in two tiers if necessary, one for privacy, the other to let in the light.

● *Tired old towels* Jazz up old white towels you cannot afford to change by adding a border of contrasting colour, say pink, or green, or use both colours, all round the edges. This will also restore the chic to towels with frayed and dog-eared edges from too much washing.

● *Unsightly plumbing* Hide unsightly pipes below washbasins with a cupboard or closet which will also be useful for extra storage. If you cannot build such a cupboard, shirr fabric on a rod, gathering tape, or stretch wire and fix it around the basin. Hide other pipes by boxing them in if you can. The resulting ledge can be used to stand things on. Alternatively you can make a feature of them with bright paint.

● *Bath that's seen better days* Cover bath panels with carpet to match the one on the floor. Or tile them. Or paste them with vinyl paper or wallpaper protected with at least two coats of polyurethane (test the paper first to make sure that it does not run. If it does, you could try covering it with a protective film of clear Fablon). If there is not a bath panel to cover, you can always make one by boxing in the bath with plywood, leaving a deep shelf all around which can either be tiled or covered in plastic laminate and used to hold objects, bottles and jars. This will also give the effect of having a luxurious built-in bath.

● An extension of the above idea is to frame both bath and basin with mahogany panelling to give a semblance of Edwardian opulence. Get a carpenter to fit neatly panelled wood sides (or do it yourself, fixing the real thing if you can afford it or staining the wood mahogany and polishing and lacquering it if you cannot).

● *No atmosphere* Create it. Add a small set of shelves for books (best covered in clear plastic like Fablon's Coveron) or objects, or collectables,

THE BATHROOM IS A ROOM TOO

Left: Mahogany-stained wood was used to make the vanity unit and panelled doors and bath panel as well as to frame the mirror. Doors are filled in with alternate panes of mirror and obscured glass for reflection, extra light and privacy. Rose and cream mini-print wallpaper was given a coat of clear eggshell varnish for extra toughness and goes well with the blue and off-white Brussels Weave Carpet.

Above: You can, of course, recess basins into almost any sort of unit, including a pine chest of drawers as here. The drawers provide instant storage facilities.

or small plants or an interesting mixture. Bring in a cane table and a cane or wicker chair and spray them white or leave them natural, and cover a cushion or two with towelling to match the towels you are using. Have a small table drawn up near the WC with piles of magazines. Keep a bottle of mineral water near the bath together with a glass.

● *Lacks luxury* Pile a glass dish or brandy balloon with pretty soaps in an appropriate colour. Decant bath salts and oils into beautiful glass jars or carafes. Let it *smell* expensive – perfume, oil, talc. Even if you just manage to buy some really luxurious deep-pile towels in a beautiful colour or a few china or brightly coloured plastic accessories, you'll be amazed at the difference such small touches make.

Family bathrooms can still look good

With the best will in the world it is almost impossible to keep a family bathroom looking tidy and elegant. All too often, towels are dropped in a soggy heap, bath toys are left lying around or stranded like sea flotsam in dry baths. Shelves are filled with a litter of ancient toothbrushes and half-finished tubes of toothpaste. Shower curtains have gone mouldy at the bottom and bath edges are thick with mostly-finished bottles, jars and tubes. It is a sorry sight. What can you do about it?

How to foresee – and forestall – eyesores

Abandon all thoughts of using wallpaper or wallcovering in a room used by a multi-generational family; it will get splashed and start to look forlorn in no time. Much better to tile all over or use plastic laminate or even paint such an area.

Fit in as much storage as possible; children and teenagers are invariably untidy. See that there are places where bath toys can be stashed away when not in use, where cleaning things can be within easy reach but out of sight and where unsightly clobber can be hidden away.

Fit a glass partition rather than a shower curtain which can get shabby or at least disarranged all too quickly.

Have separate and distinctive tooth mugs, face flannels and towels in co-ordinated colours for each member of the family – they won't look a mess, or get muddled.

Try to double the amount of heated towel rail space or have a long radiator with a rod going all the length of one wall. This way towels will at least dry quickly.

Put up hooks everywhere: on the back of the door; by the bath (for face cloths); by the basin or basins for hand towels.

Try to have double medicine cabinets, or a whole wall of cabinets like a kitchen. In fact, kitchen cabinets might be a very good idea if you have the wall space. Some manufacturers make cabinets that will go in any room.

Kitchen units maximise storage space

Perspex screens are tidier than curtains and don't rot

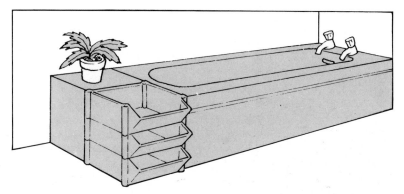

Fit storage units at end of bath

Whether you are re-modelling a bathroom or starting one from scratch there is a huge range of equipment available from the most luxurious to the purely functional.

Don't just go out and buy a bath without arming yourself first with as much information as possible. These days there are oval baths, octagonal baths, corner baths, curved baths, copies of old baths on claw feet . . . you name it . . . the choice is tremendous, not to say bewildering. So do your homework, research the market and shop around to see what's available. Remember too, that for those who are able to afford the money and the space there are now steam baths, whirlpool massage baths, shower massagers, hot tubs, jacuzzis and baths big enough for two, any of which will add to the sybaritic possibilities of your bathroom.

Basically, the more conventional baths are 1700 mm (5 ft 6 in) long by 700 mm (2 ft 3 in) wide but you can buy many other shapes including lengths from 1475 mm (4 ft 11 in) to 1800 mm (5 ft 11 in–6 ft) in widths from 700 mm (2 ft 3 in) to 8000 mm (2 ft 7$\frac{1}{2}$ in). If space is very tight you can find corner baths or sitting rather than lying baths which measure

about 1375 mm (4 ft 7 in) by 710 mm (2 ft 4 in) or 120 mm (4 ft) square; or extra deep baths or shower trays which can be used for both showering and bathing. It's important to take note of these measurements when planning a space where every inch may count. Before ordering decide exactly where you want your fixtures placed; this will determine the size of the space you have to play with and the type of bath you can fit in and still have room to manoeuvre.

More often than not, baths are fitted against a wall, tight up to a corner, but if both your space and your plumbing runs and waste pipes can stand it, you could plan for one to be centred along a wall or even in the middle of the floor. If you centre a bath in the middle of a long wall you can build a floor to ceiling partition at either end which will make it look built-in. This will allow a WC and bidet to be placed one side and a

Garden trellis on walls, left, is a sure-fire way to open up a room and get an instant summer look. Here it is used with a geranium print and marbled bath. In the room on the right walls covered with mirror panels make all the difference to this cramped space.

basin on the other. Add shower curtains from a track inset into the ceiling or fixed tight up to the ceiling, tie them back on either side and you immediately get a gracious look. You can achieve much the same look of a curtained-off aperture if the bath is fitted tight into one end of a small room.

Whatever the size and colour of the bath you choose, do try to get one with handles either side. You might be limber enough now but a bath is a long-term investment and you have to reckon on growing older and stiffer with the years. Also, handles are essential for small children and elderly people or people with back problems.

Baths: which material?

Acrylics The cheapest and most common material for baths is acrylic, which can be moulded easily to incorporate seats, soap dishes, bath-rests and so on. Water stays hotter in acrylic than metal baths and they are fairly resistant to knocks and chips although they can get scratches. The best way to cope with these when they happen is to make sure the surface is quite dry and to rub the scratch down with metal polish and rinse off thoroughly.

Acrylics burn easily, so avoid cigarettes in the bathroom. They can also be damaged by nail varnish, varnish remover and some dry cleaning liquids.

It is important to install them exactly to manufacturer's instructions or they may not remain rigid.

Glass fibre These baths are made of layers of glass fibre bonded together with polyester resin. They are much stronger and more rigid than the acrylic variety and come in a range of colours, including metallic and pearlized finishes.

Pressed steel These are fairly light and rigid baths with a smooth vitreous enamel coating and good wearing properties.

Cast iron This is the traditional and the classic, but expensive material for baths and still holds its own mainly because it has an excellent, fairly stain-proof and easy-to-clean finish or porcelain enamel fused onto the metal at very high temperature.

Bath surrounds

Unless your bath is in the centre of the room you absolutely must have a splash-resistant surround which is usually of tiles or plastic laminate. Some people choose to fix a sheet of clear or milky perspex, plexiglass or lucite over paint or wallpaper, but I have found that water can all too easily seep down the back. Whatever the material, the surround should be at least 500 mm (1 ft 8 in) high and come up to the ceiling if your bath

The green and white bathroom above has been made to look much more interesting with its centrally-placed bath flanked by bamboo chests, useful and decorative. The bath itself has also been made to look more substantial with its green tiled surround, which is quite wide enough to make a convenient seating ledge. Slim Venetian blinds at the window add to the neat architectural look as well as giving a pleasant filtered light.

Planning your space

When planning a new bathroom from scratch, you will have to consider whether to include the WC in the main area or install it separately elsewhere. There are points in favour of each arrangement and you should decide which is best suited to your needs.

Bear in mind that each fitting must have enough surrounding space for it to be used comfortably and easily. Allow 1100 × 700 mm (43 × 28 in)

alongside baths and 2200 mm (86 in) headroom. Wash-basins should have 200 mm (8 in) on either side and 700 mm (28 in) in front. WCs and bidets need 200 mm (8 in) either side and 600 mm (24 in) in front. For showers enclosed on three sides allow 900 × 700 mm (35 × 28 in) alongside and for enclosed showers 900 × 400 mm (35 × 16 in).

It may seem as if you need an enormous amount of space to accommodate these appliances. But as only one or two of them are likely to be used at the same time, the activity areas can easily overlap.

These layouts for different-shaped bathrooms indicate the *optimum* space around fittings

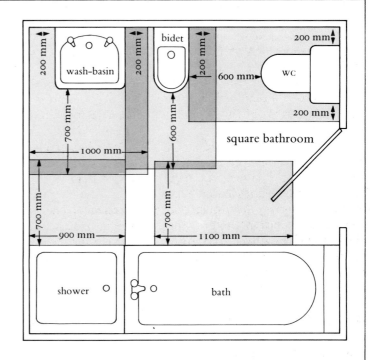

square bathroom

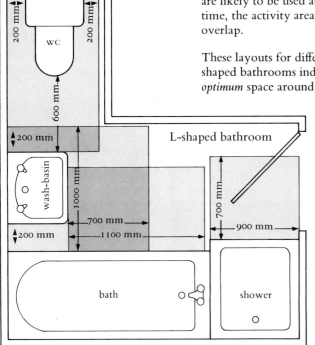

L-shaped bathroom

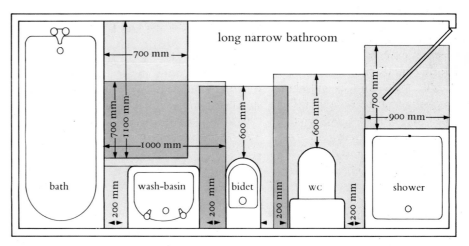

long narrow bathroom

includes a shower. The gap between bath and wall – and there will always be a slight one – should be well sealed with a ceramic tile trim, a sealing strip or a non-hardening mastic, otherwise water can trickle down and cause rot.

If you want to square off the bath you can either box it in yourself, using boarding, which you can stain, tile, carpet or laminate. If you are not handy, get a carpenter to do it, or buy ready-made front and back panels. Remember to have one removable panel so that pipes and waste can be inspected and repaired.

Save with a shower

Quite apart from being refreshing and invigorating, showers save water because they use about one-fifth of the amount needed for a bath. And they save energy, especially if you connect them to an instantaneous electric water heater which heats only the water actually used. Another advantage to a shower is that since it only takes up about one square metre (1 sq yd) of floor space it can be installed in all sorts of odd corners providing that there is a water supply and drainage near to hand and the sort of instantaneous electric heater which takes water from the mains. Otherwise the water cistern should be at least a metre (3 ft) higher than the shower head or there will not be enough pressure for the shower to work.

If you have a shower built in you will need a mixer valve and spray attachment with a thermostatic valve and a ceramic, steel or acrylic shower tray. Install them in a corner or an alcove, cover the walls with tiles and fit a glass door, glass screens or curtains according to what is appropriate to the position and your pocket. It is also very easy to put in a shower above a bath tub, again screening it off with a glass panel if that is possible with your bath design, or shower curtains. Or you can buy special shower cubicles which range tremendously in price.

Basins

You can buy free-standing pedestal wash basins, wall hung basins, basins partially supported by front legs, or basins that can be sunk into counter tops or vanity units. Like baths, they are available in porcelain enamel over cast iron, acrylic, glass fibre or in the popular vitreous china. They can be oval, round, square, rectangular, corner-shaped or shell-shaped and range in size from the small 300 mm (1 ft) widths to around 750 mm (2 ft 6 in) or more. They come in the same range of colours as baths or they can be decorated in some way. It is often sensible in a family bathroom to have two basins set side by side in a counter or vanity unit which can be made from plywood or other wood, then either stained, polished and

lacquered or covered with tiles or a laminate like Formica. More lavish counters can be made from marble or slate or stone.

Choose your taps and hardware at the same time as you order your bath. Again, there is an enormous choice to suit all tastes and pockets. The cheapest place to have taps installed is at the end of the bath and above the waste. You can choose between a pop-up waste (controlled by a lever or handle of some sort) or a plug and chain. But you can, of course, buy baths without tap holes to use with wall-mounted taps, or with separate function taps – the spout at one place, the controls in another.

WCs

WCs are generally wall-hung or the pedestal variety and can come as low as 230 mm (9 in) from the ground or considerably higher and in a variety of widths. Wooden seats are popular again, or you can buy seats to match the lavatory colour.

Bidets

If there is room, bidets should definitely be included in bathroom fixtures. They should be as near the WC as possible and, generally take up about 350 mm (1 ft 2 in). Again, you can buy them in the same colours as baths and WCs or in white. If possible, choose one with a built-in douche spray.

Top right: Bath, WC and washbasin look very much built-in in this substantial terracotta tiled and mirrored room. Note how an access door has been concealed under the basin.

Far right: Shiny black paint and a white vinyl floor give a literally smart-as-paint background to the interestingly moulded bases of bidet and basin. Their curved lines are echoed by the Michelin man perched above the rounded laundry basket, by the round mirror and light, rounded plastic storage unit and the picture of lights above the bath whose colours look more intense against the black and white scheme.

Centre: The deep round porthole mirror above the basin here has convex glass to expand the view. The thoughtfully-placed shower is ideal for hair washing.

Near right: Tongue-and-groove wood lines all the walls in a nice uncluttered room. The smooth surfaces conceal generous storage space as well as providing support for a shower stall. The cork-and-vinyl floor looks equally handsome as well as being warmly practical.

EQUIPMENT AND LAYOUT

Bathroom equipment

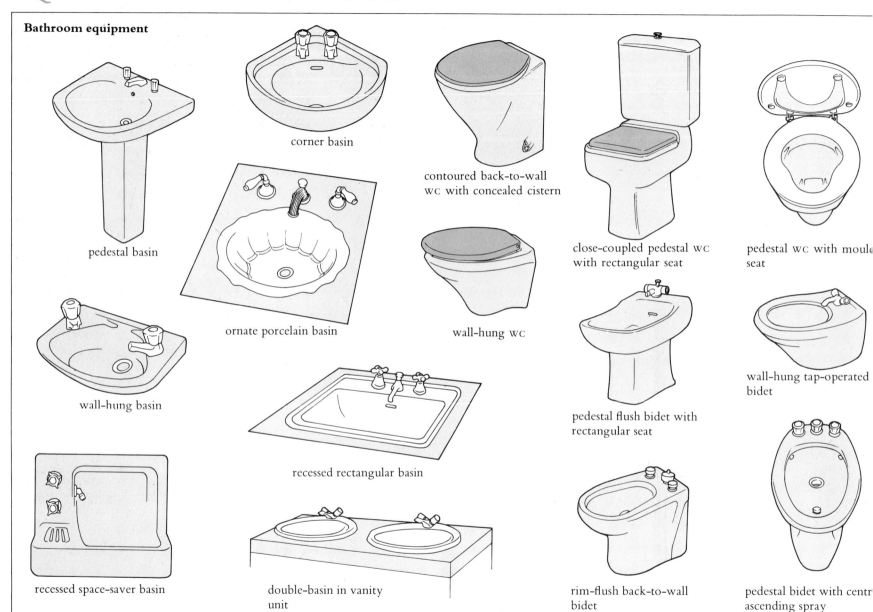

pedestal basin

corner basin

ornate porcelain basin

wall-hung basin

recessed rectangular basin

recessed space-saver basin

double-basin in vanity unit

contoured back-to-wall wc with concealed cistern

wall-hung wc

close-coupled pedestal wc with rectangular seat

pedestal flush bidet with rectangular seat

rim-flush back-to-wall bidet

pedestal wc with mould seat

wall-hung tap-operated bidet

pedestal bidet with centr ascending spray

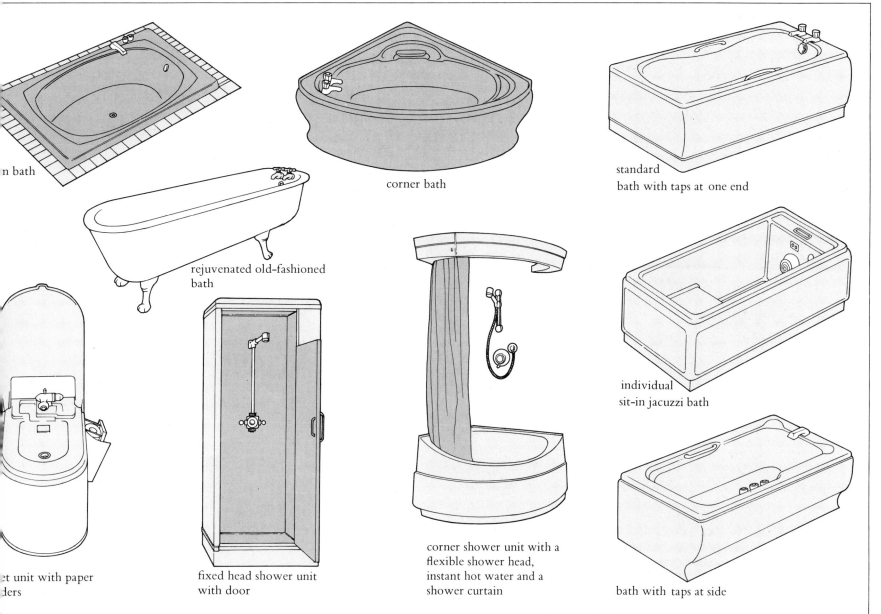

n bath

corner bath

standard
bath with taps at one end

rejuvenated old-fashioned
bath

individual
sit-in jacuzzi bath

et unit with paper
ders

fixed head shower unit
with door

corner shower unit with a
flexible shower head,
instant hot water and a
shower curtain

bath with taps at side

113

Working out

This is a bathroom for the fitness freak: half bathroom and half home gym. Functional, with its exercise bicycle and wooden bars, yet sumptuous with those same parallel bars stretched across panels of mirror, and undeniably comfortable—the deep tiled bath and shower recess, the twin basins, pine-boarded walls and sense of space make sure of that. If fitness is important to you, and you have the space and the money, such a room would be a wonderfully luxurious asset to your well-being. Colours are kept to a minimum and confined to towels and the odd accessory like the plants in their terracotta pots. Lights are spaced all around the room just under the ceiling and the room is further defined by the neat walkway of white tiles all around the wood block floor. There is a panel of mirror by the bath and, together with the others behind the parallel bars, it provides lots of extra light and sparkle as well as reflection. The whole area with its clean lines, its whiteness and its wood, has an air of wholesomeness and health totally in keeping with its twin functions. And it manages to be a remarkably handsome room as well as thoroughly practical.

atmospheric
wall lights

mirrors over bath and basin cut
in arches to reflect 30s style

peachy
rag-rubbed walls

glamorous
festoon blinds

*Cupboards either side of the bath
form a good-looking alcove in a
peachy rag-rubbed room. The
splashback has been lined with thin
marble tiles and these combined
with the specially cut arched
mirrors over the bath and basin
(seen in detail in inset) give a
rather Thirties charm. This
impression is reinforced by the
shape of the wall light, the woven
basket chair and festoon blinds.
More useful storage space has been
incorporated under the washbasin so
that clutter is hidden.*

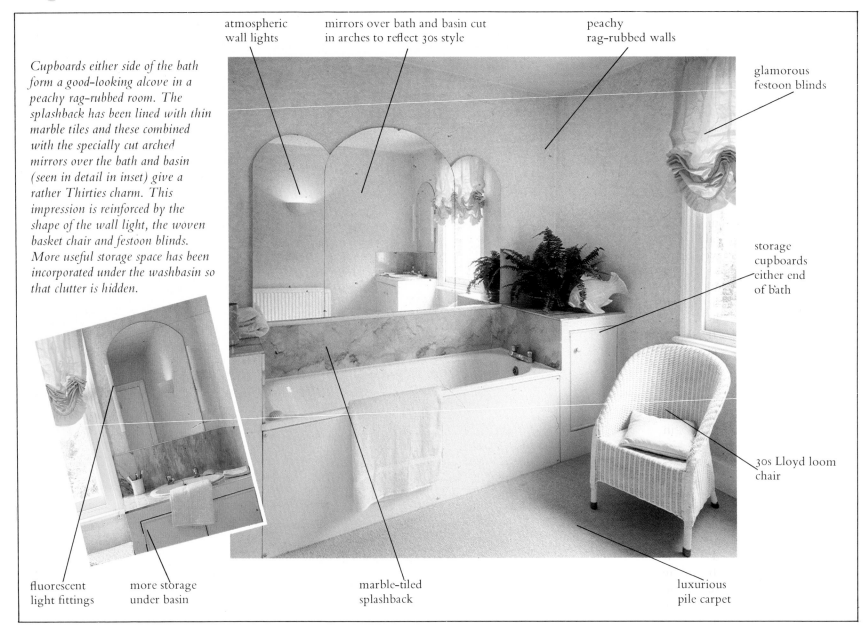

storage
cupboards
either end
of bath

30s Lloyd loom
chair

fluorescent
light fittings

more storage
under basin

marble-tiled
splashback

luxurious
pile carpet

Neat and tidy storage

Bathroom storage is generally a real headache – especially storage in a family bathroom. Medicines and medicaments, powders, soaps, toothpastes and toothbrushes, razors, personal electric equipment, shampoos, bath oils and salts, tissues, cotton wool, cleaning accessories, bath toys, toilet paper, towels and wash cloths all have to be accommodated somewhere, somehow, since they cannot all crowd the counter top and bath surrounds. The conventional medicine cabinet is hardly big enough and yet there seems no other space in the standard box-shaped bathroom. Where do you go from here? For a start, if you have not already got a built-in basin or vanity unit what about that area? It's a good space for a cupboard which will also cover any previously exposed pipes. You can always curtain-off a basin and hide a multitude of stuff behind the fabric; it isn't very difficult to fix a skirt to the basin itself. You should allow double the measurement of the basin in material. Turn over the fabric at the top and run a gathering string through it. Buy some 'gripper tape' or Velcro and glue it to the bottom of the basin. Sew exactly the same amount of tape onto the gathered skirt and clamp it to the tape on the basin. Or buy some stretch wire, run it through the top hem of the fabric and attach it to the wall either side of the basin.

Tiny bathrooms

When space is at a premium such desperate situations call for desperate measures. See if there's room for shelves or cupboards in all sorts of unexpected places. What about above the window or door or toilet or at the end of the bath? You only need narrow shelves on the whole so the smallest alcove could be used up and given a door too, if you like. If space is very tight think about fixing shelves on the backs of cupboard doors.

Corners are always possible either for an old corner cupboard, for floor-standing étagères in wood or cane, or for narrow cabinets set at right angles. Always fix a couple of hooks to the back of doors and have plenty of towel hanging space: at least one heated towel rail if there is room or a long pole over a radiator as well as hooks or rods near the basin for hand towels.

Right: Eighteen inches or so of wall depth have been stolen here to turn into a handsome mirror-lined alcove surrounded by a whole range of top and bottom storage cupboards. The other side of the room (reflected in the mirror) has been similarly treated with open shelves for towels as well as a full length linen cupboard. The neutral print wallpaper on walls, doors and ceiling harmonizes with the cream-painted dado and bath panel and is offset by the towels.

117

In this elegant room, top left, shiny pink and white paint, and a white tiled floor are set off by glamorous-looking wall sconces, neat white shutters and, best of all, a chaise-longue. The tiny cloakroom, above, is prettied up with a heart-printed vinyl wallpaper and scalloped pelmets for blind and light. The deliberately uneven wood panelling used to line the walls, bottom left, has a pleasantly rustic effect as well as being practical. Green carpet and towels make a good contrast.

Floor and wall treatments

Obviously in a bathroom you have to think first and foremost about surfaces that are resistant to steam and water. Ceramic tiles are clearly very practical for both surfaces: with a high glaze for walls and a skid-proof surface for floors. But you could also use quarry tiles, earthen-ware tiles like Mexican and Portu-guese, and glass bricks or mosaic. I once saw a small bathroom entirely covered – ceiling as well – with mirrored mosaic tiles and the effect was stupendous.

Cheapest of course, is paint which is best in an eggshell or high gloss finish. Wallpaper looks good, but must be applied above a good run of tiles around bath and basin, or else covered in clear perspex or plexiglass or glass around the damp prone areas. Vinyl and vinyl-coated papers are practical. Another good idea is to paint over any bathroom wallpaper with a clear eggshell glaze like polyurethane. This will preserve the paper for a far longer time.

You can apply laminated panels of hardboard with a baked-on plastic coating in a large range of colours and finishes including a realistic marble. Formica make an excellent range of panels that can be applied straight to the walls as well as to counter tops, and then there is the real McCoy – marble itself – which now comes in 12 mm ($\frac{1}{2}$ in) thick veneers for floors, walls and other surfaces. If you don't mind the occasional steaming-up, mirror-lined walls look very glamorous and will also expand the space. Wood panelling or tongue-and-groove boarding with a coating of poly-urethane looks warm and interest-ing, as do nice wood floors.

Vinyl-coated cork is a popular choice for floors and so are vinyl tiles, resilient sheet flooring and the new fibre carpets and carpet tiles which are more practical than wool in a wettish environment. Cotton tumble twist comes in a large range of colours and lifts up easily to shake, clean or put in the washing machine. If areas around bath and basin are very well protected and occupants are reasonably docile in the bath and shower, wallcoverings like felt or wool, cotton, hessian or burlap can look warm and smart. So too could lengths of towelling stapled to the wall with the cut edges covered in a braid or beading.

Right: Pirelli rubber stud flooring, which is fairly inexpensive, lines the floor and walls of this platformed sunken bath area. Other walls are laid with plain white tiles and the lower half of the room is carpeted. This contrast of textures, colour and finish is heightened by the slim white slats of the blinds, (which also serve to separate off the bath area from the rest of the room), the plants, baskets and figured lights.

EQUIPMENT AND LAYOUT

Window dressing

Bathroom windows are generally small so can lend themselves to quite lavish treatments that might not be affordable on larger windows. If you are not overlooked you can use tied-back curtains or festoon or Austrian blinds in muslins, laces, light cottons or broderie Anglaise for a particularly pretty look. If you want to disguise ugly bobbly bathroom glass which you cannot replace, try using café curtains, or translucent net, or white holland blinds. Matchstick or bamboo blinds can look good, so can Venetian and wooden louvred blinds. Shutters, especially the adjustable variety look very fresh and rural. Again, if you are not overlooked, you could try leaving the windows bare and just standing plants or a row of glasses on the window sill. Another idea is to fill the window frame with narrow glass shelves on which you can mass

Left: Sweeping lace curtains frame both bath and window in a nicely unusual country bathroom with its old-fashioned claw-foot bath and china jardinière. Bountiful plants provide almost as much green inside as can be seen through the window. The romantic window treatment has the added effect of literally framing the thoroughly pleasing view outside. The gentle feel is helped by the Edwardian light shade and warm cork floor tiles which blend with the wood.

plants or coloured glasses or blue and white jugs or what you will.

If you do have a big or biggish window, treat it like a living room or bedroom and use a blind with tied-back dress curtains. And if you do have an otherwise slickly-tiled bathroom, the way you dress the window will make all the difference between an impersonal space and an interesting one.

Choosing accessories

There can hardly have been a better time than now for buying pretty bathroom accessories, so there's no excuse for not being able to titivate the plainest little space even if – as in rented accommodation – you can-not change equipment, walls or lay-out. Take towels – they can be worth their weight in gold. Look for the sort of colours that will make an unfortunate shade in equipment or tiles look much more integrated, or buy towels to match or contrast with a predominant colour on walls or floor.

Buy matching porcelain tooth-mugs and soap dishes, tissue holders and cotton wool jars, cache pots and paper holders. To update a very plain cold space look for those large primary coloured hooks and rails, mugs and holders, or find accessories in pine or brass or clear perspex or plexiglass. These sort of vivid, eye-catching accents can make a dull bathroom seem lively and friendly.

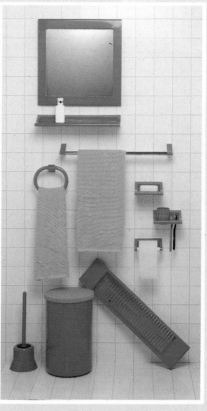

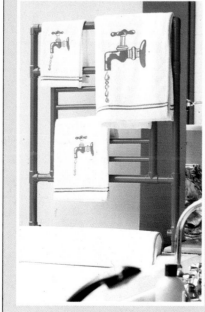

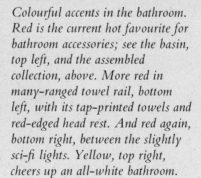

Colourful accents in the bathroom. Red is the current hot favourite for bathroom accessories; see the basin, top left, and the assembled collection, above. More red in many-ranged towel rail, bottom left, with its tap-printed towels and red-edged head rest. And red again, bottom right, between the slightly sci-fi lights. Yellow, top right, cheers up an all-white bathroom.

EQUIPMENT AND LAYOUT

Heat and light

Warmth is important

One of the most important ingredients for comfort in a bathroom is getting it the right temperature: cosily warm in winter and cool enough in summer. If you can possibly have a heated towel rail you should do so, but beware of one that is run solely off the central heating system. This is fine when the heating is chugging away, but what about when it is not? To make sure of warm dry towels at all times try to get one run off the hot water system itself, or have a supplementary electrically-heated rail, or just an electric rack. If your hot water tank is placed in a cupboard in the bathroom this will also help to keep the room warm as well as making an extra drying place for towels. If you do not have a radiator of some sort, extra warmth can be provided by a wall-mounted fan or an infra red heater mounted above the door or above the mirror.

If you have to have an electric water heater in the bathroom it is worth knowing that you can buy it in the form of a cabinet with a mirror front which looks neater than the old tank-shaped variety.

Avoiding condensation

Condensation which can be such a nuisance in bathrooms, steaming up the mirrors and windows, can usu-ally be avoided to a great extent by steady warmth and adequate ventilation. If you do not want to open a window in winter, you can install an extractor fan on the wall or in the window itself. And the sort of extractor fan that is obligatory in all internal bathrooms will automatically keep a room free from fogging. Mirrors with built-in lights which warm the glass will also eliminate condensation.

The best sort of lighting

If your room is very small, the best solution for general light is a central ceiling fixture, for this, like the kitchen, or utility room, is the one place in the home where you don't particularly want mood lighting.

Lights either side of the mirror or all around as for theatrical dressing rooms are best for make-up and shaving, or just above if only for shaving. You can buy mirrors with strips of bulbs all around or at the top, or you can buy separate strips to superimpose yourself.

If you have a large room, perhaps a bath-dressing-room, bath-study, you can conceal strip lights behind curtains or window treatments of whatever sort, recess spots into the ceiling (if you have a reasonable recess) to pin-point particular objects or plants, or install waterproof downlights and control the whole system with a dimmer switch for glamour. If you have an internal bathroom, you might also consider some of the luminous ceilings available, or try putting light up behind a floating false ceiling – which is also a good idea for any small dark bathroom, with or without windows.

Safety factors

It is absolutely essential that you do not use any electric appliances near water. Radiant electric fires must be placed high up on a wall and switched on or off by a cord; lights should preferably be controlled either by switches outside the room or by further cords. Wet hands that come into contact with switches result in tragedy. Never iron in the bathroom and don't dry your hair with an electric hair dryer there or use any other electric appliance.

Above: Warm, wood-lined walls and bath panel never suffer from the effects of condensation. Two ideas worth noting are the bath set at an angle from the corner and the continuous towel rail running all round the room above the radiator so that lots of towels can dry at once. Matting on the floor allied to the wood adds to the sporty training-room feeling.

Right: Recessed ceiling lights and theatrical bulbs above the dressing-table (reflected in mirror) give excellent overall and make-up/shaving light in this attractive and spacious looking bathroom. Heat is provided by a wall-mounted radiator which also serves to warm the towels.

Accent lighting Decorative lighting which is used to draw attention to chosen objects, and to create moods and highlights.

Architrave A moulded or decorated band framing a panel or an opening such as a door or window.

Austrian blind Arched blind similar to a festoon blind or pull-up curtain. It has rows of vertical shirring and can be raised and lowered by cords threaded through rings at the back of the blind.

Baldachin A draped canopy like those used over pulpits and altars.

Balloon blind This has deep inverted pleats which create a billowing balloon-like effect.

Batiste A fine fabric like cambric.

Burlap A coarse sacking material also known as hessian.

Butt-edged Two edges which meet but do not overlap.

Café curtain A short curtain hung from a rod suspended halfway down a window, as in French cafés. It is sometimes hung in a double tier, and is a useful treatment for windows that open outwards or face the street.

Cantilever A projection from the wall.

Casement window A window that opens on vertical hinges.

Corian A marble-like plastic substance used for sinks and worktops. It can be moulded to form a continuous work surface, and is durable and almost completely stain-resistant.

Cornice A decorative, horizontal band of plaster, metal or wood used to surmount a wall or to conceal curtain fixtures.

Corona A crown-shaped projection above the bed from which drapery is hung.

Coving A curved moulding connecting the ceiling and wall.

Dado The lower part of a wall where separated by a rail known as the dado rail.

Dimmer switch A knob (or rheostat) or panel that is used to control brightness of light. It saves energy as well as giving a flexible range of lighting levels.

Dormer window A vertical window set into a sloping roof.

Downlights Fitting which can be mounted on, or recessed into a ceiling to cast pools of light onto the surface below. Most are fitted with an antiglare device, and the direction of light can be controlled with a baffle.

Dragging A paint technique which gives a subtle effect to a large wall surface. Paint is applied in a thin wash in vertical strokes with an almost dry brush in a contrasting shade to the base coat.

Etagère A set of open shelves supported by columns or corner posts.

Festoon blind Similar to an Austrian blind but rather more elaborate.

Grasscloth A fine soft fabric made from the fibres of the inner bark of an eastern plant.

Grouting Filling up or finishing joints between tiles with a thin mortar.

Half-tester A small canopy or tester (q.v.) over a bed, covering only the pillow end.

Hessian A coarsely woven cloth.

Laminate A very strong multi-layered material.

Louvres A series of overlapping slats which filter or exclude light while allowing ventilation. Fitted in frames they are used for doors, screens and shutters.

Marbling A paint technique which gives a veined, marble-like appearance to a surface.

Moiré The wavy design on silk or other fabrics, which gives a watered appearance.

Murphy bed A bed that lets down from the wall against which it is concealed when not in use.

Ottoman A long, low upholstered seat with no back, or a circular seat divided into four with a central back.

Pelmet or valance A decorative, horizontal band of fabric usually attached to the top of the window frame or just above, to hide rods and provide added interest.

Pharmacy lamp An old-fashioned lamp used in chemists' dispensaries.

Pillow shams Covers for pillows to match bed covering, when pillows are propped on top of the bed.

Pin-board A board, usually made from cork, on which papers or pictures can be attached with pins.

Pinoleum or matchstick blind A blind made from very thin wooden reeds.

Rag-rolling A paint technique in which the top coat of paint is partly removed while still wet with a roll of cloth, to reveal the base coat in a contrasting shade.

Roman blind One that draws up into neat horizontal folds by means of cords threaded through rings attached at regular intervals to the back of the fabric. On heavier fabrics, light battens can be attached to keep the folds crisp.

Shoji screen A traditional Japanese screen, made with translucent paper.

Spongeing A paint technique which gives a soft speckled effect. A sponge is used to stipple paint onto a base coat in a contrast colour.

Stencil A decorative design which is cut out of waxed paper or acetate, then reproduced onto a surface below with paint using a stencil brush or spray can.

Tester A wood or fabric canopy covering the whole bed area.

Tongue-and-groove panelling Wood panelling, where the boards are interlocked along the edges.

Truckle bed A low bed on castors or wheels for rolling under another bed.

Uplights Accent lights which are placed on the floor. They can be concealed behind sofas and plants to give dramatic effects.

Valance or pelmet A decorative horizontal band of fabric usually attached to the top of the window frame, or just above, to hide rods and provide added interest.

Vanity unit A storage unit which encloses the basin.

Venetian blind A pull-up blind made with horizontal slats that can be adjusted to let in or exclude light.

Wash stand A piece of furniture which holds the basin.

Yacht paint A tough, hard-wearing paint, also known as deck paint, used on boats or to paint wood floors.

ACKNOWLEDGMENTS

The author and publishers would like particularly to thank the following people and companies for their contribution to this book:

for their invaluable help and research work: Pamela Gough, Virginia Bredin

for technical advice: David Champion, Colour Counsellors Ltd, Deborah Evans, Shirley Heron

for allowing us to photograph their homes: Felicity Bozanquet, Virginia Bredin, Fenella Brown, Francesca Fennymore, Oliver Gallagher, Felicity Green, Jane & Caradoc King, Dieter Klein, Sandy Kom Losy, Daniel & Lily Morocco, Jancis Robinson, Anna Southall & Chris Searle

for supplying merchandise for the room sets: Judy Afia's Carpet Shop, Amtico, Bernstein & Banleys Ltd, Brintons Carpets Ltd, The Conran Shop, Designers Guild, Domus Decor Ltd, Mary Fox Linton Ltd, Gaskell Broadloom Carpets Ltd, Liberty, Marks & Spencer plc, Osborne & Little Ltd, Helen Sheane Wallcoverings Ltd, Tissunique Ltd, Waldorf Carpets, World's End Tiles & Flooring Ltd

for supplying props for special photography: Albany Linens, And So To Bed, Descamps Ltd, Designers Guild, Le Cadeau, Covent Garden, Lunn Antiques, Mary Fox Linton, ICTC, Marks & Spencer plc, Sanderson Ltd, Christopher Wray's Lighting Emporium

Black and white line illustrations by Ed Roberts/Tudor Art Studios. Colour illustrations by Ross Wardle/Tudor Art Studios.

Special photography

Jon Bouchier 10 above left, 14 above left (designer Dieter Klein), 16 left, 21, 23 centre and left (designer Lenny), 32 left and right (designer Anthony Collett), 41, 47 (designer Anthony Collett), 58, 91 above and below left (designer Fenella Brown), 94 (designer Dieter Klein), 96 above right, 100 left and right, 101 (designer Lenny), 116 left and right (designer Jane King), 123.

Jessica Strang 10 above centre, 14 below left, 28, 29 right, 117.

The publishers would like to thank the following organizations and individuals for their kind permission to reproduce the photographs in this book: Acme Wardrobes 65; Jon Bouchier/EWA 20 below right (designer Ian Allen), 111 below left; Michael Boys/Susan Griggs Agency Ltd. 31, 33 below centre, 37, 40 above right, 44 right, 50, 71 right, 77 below right, 84, 95 below left; Camera Press 11, 63 below centre, 72 centre and right, 77 above left, 78, 82 left, 91 above right, 93, 95 above left, 121 above left; Cover Plus Paints 111 right; Crayonne 121 above left and above centre; David Cripps/EWA 34 below left; Mike Crockett/EWA 10 below left, 16 right, 85 left; Crown Wallcoverings 63 above centre; Michael Datoli 49, 57; Designers Guild 51 above right, 63 below left, 68; Michael Dunne 6, 8, 17, 18, 22 left, 30, 33 above centre, 34 above right and left, 35 left, 44 left, 48 above left, 59 above left and right, 70 above right, 77 above right, 86, 104 left, 106, 118 above right; Leonardo Ferrante 75 below right; c. Peter M. Fine 1983 118 below left; Formica Ltd. 64; Christine Hanscomb 20 above right, 48 below left, 120; Clive Helm/EWA 19 (designer Jennifer Granville Dixon), 39, 107 (designer Campbell Pelner); Graham Henderson/EWA 33 above right, 85 (designer Nicolas Hills), Ken Kirkwood 27 left and right; Mary Fox Linton 75 above right; Neil Lorimer/EWA 63 above right, 77 below left; Mayfair Mix and Match Collection 59 below left; Chris Mead 9, 40 below right, 54; Michael Nicholson/EWA 20 below left (designer Virginia Bates), 22 right (designer Chester Jones), 29 left (designer Maggi Heany), 34 below right, 35 right, 48 below right (designer Coombe Manor Fabric), 51 below right (designer Dorit Egli), 52 above left (designer Tricia Guild), 55, 91 below right (designer Elizabeth Dickson), 102 right, 103, 111 above left (designer Twyfords), 118 above left, 121 below right (designer Campbell Zogolovitch), Max Pike's Bathroom Shop and Whirlpool Centre 121 below left; Arthur Sanderson Ltd. Upstairs Collection 51 above centre; Jessica Strang 51 above left, 70 below right, 73 (designer Britta Morse), 82 above and below right (designer J. Strang), 87 (designer Antonia Graham), 96 below centre (designer Ann Mollo), 104 right, 111 below centre, 122 (designer Lou and Mei-Lou Klein); Tim Street-Porter/EWA 52 below left (designer Rosen), 53 (designer Frank Gehry), 76; Sunway Blinds Ltd. 108; Syndication International 63 above left, 119; Transworld Feature Syndicate 71 left, 92, 96 left (Elyse Lewin), 96 below right; Zenith Windows Ltd. 79.

INDEX